SpringerBriefs in Computer Science

T0235631

Editors

Stan Zdonik

Shashi Shekhar

Jonathan Katz

Xindong Wu

Lakhmi C. Jain

David Padua

Xuemin (Sherman) Shen

Borko Furht

V.S. Subrahmanian

Martial Hebert

Katsushi Ikeuchi

Bruno Siciliano

Sushil Jajodia

More information about this series at http://www.springer.com/series/10028

Soharab Hossain Shaikh • Khalid Saeed
Nabendu Chaki

Moving Object Detection Using Background Subtraction

Springer

Soharab Hossain Shaikh
A K Choudhury School of Information
   Technology
University of Calcutta
Kolkata
India

Khalid Saeed
Faculty of Computer Science
Bialystok University of Technology
Bialystok
Poland

Physics and Applied Computer Science
AGH University of Science and Technology
Krakow
Poland

Nabendu Chaki
Department of Computer Science
   and Engineering
University of Calcutta
Kolkata
India

ISSN 2191-5768 ISSN 2191-5776 (electronic)
ISBN 978-3-319-07385-9 ISBN 978-3-319-07386-6 (eBook)
DOI 10.1007/978-3-319-07386-6
Springer Cham Heidelberg New York Dordrecht London

Library of Congress Control Number: 2014940731

Springer is part of Springer Science + Business Media (www.springer.com)

To my wife Sukanya, for her constant support and encouragement in all my endeavours.

Soharab Hossain Shaikh

To my Parents, my Wife Alicja, Daughter Aida and Son Emil.

Khalid Saeed

To Shantibrata Majumdar, Sarmila Roy, and Madhumita Mitra—my elder brother and sisters, who have kept my childhood colourful.

Nabendu Chaki

Contents

About the Authors

Soharab Hossain Shaikh is a faculty member at A. K. Choudhury School of Information Technology, University of Calcutta, India. After receiving the B.Sc. degree with Honors in Computer Science from University of Calcutta in 2001, he has completed M. Sc. in Computer and Information Science in 2003 followed by M. Tech. in Computer Science and Engineering in 2005 from the Department of Computer Science and Engineering, University of Calcutta. He has received a fellowship from the Italian Ministry of Education for Universities and Research (MIUR) for perusing research work at Ca'Foscari, University of Venice, Italy in 2006–2007. His research interest includes image processing, computer vision, biometrics and pattern recognition. He works in active collaboration with AGH University of Science and Technology, Bialystok Technical University, Poland. He jointly holds a US-patent on Character Recognition and coauthored a book entitled *Exploring Image Binarization Techniques* with Springer India. Mr. Shaikh has published a number of research papers in various international conferences and journal. He has recently submitted Ph.D in the domain of computer vision and image processing. He has served as reviewer/committee member in a number of international conferences/symposiums and journals. He is also a member of IEEE Computer Society and ACM, Kolkata.

Khalid Saeed received the BSc Degree in Electrical and Electronics Engineering in 1976 from Baghdad University in 1976, the MSc and PhD Degrees from Wroclaw University of Technology, in Poland in 1978 and 1981, respectively. He received his DSc Degree (Habilitation) in Computer Science from Polish Academy of Sciences in Warsaw in 2007. He is a Professor of Computer Science with AGH University of Science and Technology in Poland. He has published more than 200 publications—edited 23 books, Journals and Conference

Proceedings, 8 text and reference books. He supervised more than 110 MSc and 12 PhD theses. His areas of interest are *Biometrics, Image Analysis and Processing and Computer Information Systems*. He gave 39 *invited lectures and keynotes in different universities in Europe, China, India, South Korea and Japan*. The talks were on *Biometric Image Processing* and *Analysis*. He received about 18 academic awards. Khalid Saeed is a member of more than 15 editorial boards of international journals and conferences. He is an IEEE Senior Member and has been selected as *IEEE Distinguished Speaker for 2011–2016*. Khalid Saeed is the *Editor-in-Chief of International Journal of Biometrics with Inderscience Publishers*.

Nabendu Chaki is a Senior Member of IEEE and an Associate Professor in the Department Computer Science & Engineering, University of Calcutta, India. Besides editing several volumes in Springer in LNCS and other series, Nabendu has authored three text books with reputed publishers like Taylor and Francis (CRC Press), Pearson Education, etc. Dr. Chaki has published more than 120 refereed research papers in Journals and International conferences. His areas of research interests include image processing, distributed systems, and network security. Dr. Chaki has also served as a Research Assistant Professor in the Ph.D. program in Software Engineering in U.S. Naval Postgraduate School, Monterey, CA. He is a visiting faculty member for many Universities including the University of Ca'Foscari, Venice, Italy. Dr. Chaki has contributed in SWEBOK v3 of the IEEE Computer Society as a Knowledge Area Editor for Mathematical Foundations. Besides being in the editorial board for of Springer and many international journals, he has also served in the committees of more than 50 international conferences. He is the founding Chapter Chair for ACM Professional Chapter in Kolkata, India since January 2014.

Chapter 1
Introduction

1.1 Video Processing, Object Detection and Tracking

A video or movie is a collection of static images or frames and associated audio data. A frame is a single picture or still shot, that is shown as part of a larger video or movie. Many single pictures are run in quick succession to produce what appears to be a seamless video. Therefore, a video consists of a sequence of static images or frames. In a video, images are captured at a fixed rate (25–30 fps or 60 fps) depending on the capturing speed of the camera. A camera with a specification of 30 fps means that 30 still frames are captured per second to form a video stream. These frames can be extracted from a video stream and processed in a similar manner in which an image is processed. All image processing operations can be performed on an extracted frame.

Object detection in videos involves verifying the presence of an object in image sequences and possibly locating it precisely for recognition. Object detection is closely related to another task in computer vision called tracking of the objects. As stated earlier, a video is actually a sequence of images (frames) displayed in a quick succession so that human eyes can percept the continuity of its content. It is quite obvious that all image processing techniques can be applied to individual frames extracted from a video. The contents of two consecutive frames in a video are usually closely related.

Object tracking deals with monitoring the spatial and temporal changes of an object in a video sequence, including its presence, position, size, shape, etc. This is done by solving the temporal correspondence problem dealing with matching the target region in successive frames of a sequence of images taken at closely-spaced time intervals. These two tasks (object detection and tracking) are closely related as tracking usually starts with detection of the objects, while detecting an object repeatedly in subsequent frames in a sequence is often necessary to help and verify tracking.

Modeling of the visual contents can be done as a hierarchy of layers of abstractions; e.g. the bottom layer contains the raw pixels with brightness/color information. The next upper layer contains features such as edges, lines, corners, curves, and different colored regions in a frame. A higher abstraction layer may combine and in-

S. H. Shaikh et al., *Moving Object Detection Using Background Subtraction*,
SpringerBriefs in Computer Science, DOI 10.1007/978-3-319-07386-6_1,

terpret these features as objects and their attributes. The topmost layer contains the human level concepts involving number of objects and relationships among them.

1.2   Moving Object Detection

Moving object detection and subsequent classification and recognition of the objects is one of the fundamental interests in the field of computer vision. In moving object detection the primary objective is to analyze a video sequence to detect the objects that are in motion with respect to a background scene. In case of a stationery camera, the background is assumed to be static.

Moving object detection is done using three different kinds of approaches: optical flow [1], temporal differencing [2] and background subtraction [3, 4].

Background subtraction approaches consist of two important steps: the proper generation and updating of a reference background image, and the suitable subtraction between the current image and the background model. A number of methods have been proposed by various researchers over the years. Such methods differ mainly in the way the background model is generated and in the procedure used to update the model.

1.3   Applications of Moving Object Detection

i. Detection of moving objects from video is essential for different surveillance and security applications. This is especially required to trace an abandoned object (e.g. a briefcase) that could be a security threat, locating a vehicle in a stray area in a parking lot, intruder in a security sensitive area etc.
ii. In Human Computer Interaction (HCI) systems it is used to detect and track different body components (e.g. a moving hand for gesture recognition) for building systems that can interact with a computer in a more natural human-like manner.
iii. In gait analysis, this is used for extracting out the moving human silhouette from a video stream [5].
iv. There are various other usage of moving object detection; e.g. human activity recognition [6] and real-time object classification [7] from video.
v. Moving object detection has also found its application in medical image processing, virtual and augmented reality, robotics etc.

Bibliography

1. N. Paragios, R. Deriche; "Geodesic active contours and level sets for the detection and tracking of moving objects", IEEE Transactions on Pattern Analysis and Machine Intelligence, Vol. 22 (3), pp. 266–280, 2000.

2. S. Fejes, L.S. Davis; "Detection of independent motion using directional motion estimation", Computer Vision and Image Understanding (CVIU), Vol. 74 (2), pp. 101–120, 1999.
3. M. Piccardi; "Background subtraction techniques: A review", IEEE Int. Conf on Systems, Man and Cybernetics (SMC), Vol. 4, pp. 3199–3104, 2004.
4. S. Elhabian, K. El-Sayed, S. Ahmed; "Moving object detection in spatial domain using background removal techniques—State-of-Art", Recent Patents on Computer Science, Vol. 1, pp. 32–54, 2008.
5. S.H. Shaikh, S.K. Bhunia and N. Chaki; "On Generation of Silhouette of Moving Objects from Video"; Springer Proceedings of the 4th International Conference on Signal and Image Processing (ICSIP), Vol. 1, pp. 213–223, 2012.
6. J. M. Chaqueta, E.J. Carmonaa, A.F. Caballerob; "A survey of video datasets for human action and activity recognition", Computer Vision and Image Understanding, Vol. 117 (6), pp. 633–659, 2013.
7. Lun Zhang, Li. S.Z., X. Yuan, S. Xiang; "Real-time Object Classification in Video Surveillance Based on Appearance Learning", IEEE Conference on Computer Vision and Pattern Recognition(CVPR), pp. 1–8, 2007.

Chapter 2
Moving Object Detection Approaches, Challenges and Object Tracking

2.1 Object Detection from Video

In a video there are primarily two sources of information that can be used for detection and tracking of objects: visual features (e.g. color, texture and shape) and motion information. Robust approaches have been suggested by combining the statistical analysis of visual features and temporal analysis of motion information. A typical strategy may first segment a frame into a number of regions based on visual features like color and texture, subsequently merging of regions with similar motion vectors can be performed subject to certain constraints such as spatial neighborhood of the pixels.

A large number of methodologies have been proposed by a number of researchers focusing on the object detection from a video sequence. Most of them make use of multiple techniques and there are combinations and intersections among different methodologies. All these make it very difficult to have a uniform classification of existing approaches.

This chapter broadly classifies the different approaches available for moving object detection from video.

2.1.1 Background Subtraction

Background subtraction is a commonly used technique for motion segmentation in static scenes [1]. It attempts to detect moving regions by subtracting the current image pixel-by-pixel from a reference background image. The pixels where the difference is above a threshold are classified as foreground. The creation of the background image is known as background modeling (e.g. by averaging images over time in an initialization period). After creating a foreground pixel map, some morphological post processing operations such as erosion, dilation and closing are performed to reduce the effects of noise and enhance the detected regions. The reference background is updated with new images over time to adapt to dynamic scene changes.

S. H. Shaikh et al., *Moving Object Detection Using Background Subtraction*,
SpringerBriefs in Computer Science, DOI 10.1007/978-3-319-07386-6_2,
© The Author(s) 2014

There are different approaches to this basic scheme of background subtraction in terms of foreground region detection, background maintenance and post processing.

In [2] Heikkila and Silven uses the simple version of this scheme where a pixel at location (x, y) in the current image I_t is marked as foreground if $|I_t(x, y) - B_t(x, y)| > Th$ is satisfied; where Th is a predefined threshold.

The background image B_T is updated by the use of an Infinite Impulse Response (IIR) filter as follows:

$$B_{t+1} = \alpha I_t + (1 - \alpha) B_t$$

The foreground pixel map creation is followed by morphological closing and the elimination of small-sized regions.

Although background subtraction techniques perform well at extracting most of the relevant pixels of moving regions even they stop, they are usually sensitive to dynamic changes when, for instance, stationary objects uncover the background (e.g. a parked car moves out of the parking lot) or sudden illumination changes occur.

2.1.2 Temporal Differencing

In temporal differencing, moving regions are detected by taking pixel-by-pixel difference of consecutive frames (two or three) in a video sequence. Temporal differencing is the most common method for moving object detection in scenarios where the camera is moving. Unlike static camera segmentation, where the background is comparably stable, the background is changing along time for moving camera; therefore, it is not appropriate to build a background model in advance. Instead, the moving object is detected by taking the difference of consecutive image frames $t-1$ and t. However, the motion of the camera and the motion of the object are mixed in the moving camera. Therefore in some techniques the motion of the camera is estimated first.

This method is highly adaptive to dynamic changes in the scene as most recent frames are involved in the computation of the moving regions. However, it generally fails to detect whole relevant pixels of some types of moving objects. It also wrongly detects a trailing regions as moving object (known as ghost region) when there is an object that is moving fast in the frames. Detection will also not be correct for objects that preserve uniform regions.

A sample object for inaccurate motion detection is shown in Fig. 2.1. The mono colored region of the human body (portions of legs) makes the temporal differencing algorithm to fail in extracting all pixels of the human's moving body. The white region at the left outer contour of the human body represents the ghost region.

This method also fails to detect the objects that have stopped in the scene. This occurs due to the reason that the last frame of the video sequence is treated as the reference which is subtracted from the current frame. Additional methods should be

Fig. 2.1 Temporal frame differencing. (**a**) Present Frame (PF) (**b**) Previous Frame (Prev) (**c**) Result=PF−Prev

adopted in order to detect stopped objects. This problem may be solved by considering a background model generated taking frames that came earlier in the sequence and are temporally distant from the present frame; this will incorporate other problems in detecting recent changes in the scene).

A two-frame differencing method is presented by Lipton et al. [3] where the pixels that satisfy the following equation are marked as foreground.

$$\left| I_t(x,y) \; I_{t-1}(x,y) \right| > Th$$

In order to overcome shortcomings of two frame differencing in some cases, three frame differencing can be used [4]. For instance, Collins et al. developed a hybrid method that combines three-frame differencing with an adaptive background subtraction model [5]. The hybrid algorithm successfully segments moving regions in video without the defects of temporal differencing and background subtraction.

2.1.3   Statistical Approaches

Statistical characteristics of individual pixels have been utilized to overcome the shortcomings of basic background subtraction methods. These statistical methods are mainly inspired by the background subtraction methods in terms of keeping and dynamically updating statistics of the pixels that belong to the background image process. Foreground pixels are identified by comparing each pixel's statistics with that of the background model. This approach is becoming more popular due to its reliability in scenes that contain noise, illumination changes and shadows [4].

The statistical method proposed by Stauffer and Grimson [6] describes an adaptive background mixture model for real-time tracking. In this approach, every pixel is separately modeled by a mixture of Gaussians which are updated online by incoming image data. In order to detect whether a pixel belongs to a foreground or background process, the Gaussian distributions of the mixture model for that pixel are evaluated.

The W4 [7] system uses a statistical background model where each pixel is represented with its minimum (Min) and maximum (Max) intensity values and maximum intensity difference (Diff) between any consecutive frames observed during initial training period where the scene contains no moving objects. A pixel in the current image I_t is classified as foreground if it satisfies:

$$\left|Min(x, y) - I_t(x, y)\right| > Diff(x, y) \text{ or } \left|Max(x, y) - I_t(x, y)\right| > Diff(x, y)$$

After thresholding, a single iteration of morphological erosion is applied to the detected foreground pixels to remove one-pixel thick noise. In order to grow the eroded regions to their original sizes, a sequence of erosion and dilation is performed on the foreground pixel map. Also, small-sized regions are eliminated after applying connected component labeling to find the regions. The statistics of the background pixels that belong to the non-moving regions of current image are updated with new image data.

2.1.4   Optical Flow

Optical flow methods [8–10] make use of the flow vectors of moving objects over time to detect moving regions in an image. In this approach, the apparent velocity and direction of every pixel in the frame have to be computed. It is an effective but time consuming method. Background motion model, which serves to stabilize the image of the background plane, can be calculated using optic flow. Independent motion can also be detected by this approach as either in the form of residual flow or by the flow in the direction of the image gradient which is not predicted by the background plane motion. This method can detect motion in video sequences even from a moving camera and moving background, however, most of the optical flow methods are computationally complex and cannot be used in real-time without specialized hardware.

2.2   Challenges

Object detection and tracking remains an open research problem even after research of several years in this field. A robust, accurate and high performance approach is still a great challenge today. The difficulty level of this problem highly depends on how one defines the object to be detected and tracked.

If only a few visual features (e.g. color) are used as representation of an object, it is not so difficult to identify the all pixels with same color as the object. However, there is always a possibility of existence of another object or background with the same color information. Moreover, the change of illumination in the scene does not guarantee that the color will be same for the same object in all the frames. This leads to inaccurate segmentation based on only visual features (e.g. color). This type of variability changes is quite obvious as video objects generally are moving objects. The images of an object may change drastically as it moves from one frame to another through the field of view of a camera. This variability comes from three principle sources namely variation in target pose or deformations, variation in illumination and partial/full occlusion of the target [11].

The typical challenges of background subtraction in the context of video surveillance have been listed below:

2.2.1   Illumination Changes

It is desirable that background model adapts to gradual changes of the appearance of the environment. For example in outdoor settings, the light intensity typically varies during day. Sudden illumination changes can also occur in the scene. This type of change occurs for example with sudden switching on/off a light in a indoor environment. This may also happen in outdoor scenes (fast transition from cloudy to bright sunlight). Illumination strongly affects the appearance of background, and cause false positive detections. The background model should take this into consideration.

2.2.2   Dynamic Background

Some parts of the scenery may contain movement (a fountain, movements of clouds, swaying of tree branches, wave of water etc.), but should be regarded as background, according to their relevance. Such movement can be periodical or irregular (e.g., traffic lights, waving trees). Handling such background dynamics is a challenging task.

2.2.3   Occlusion

Occlusion (partial/full) may affect the process of computing the background frame. However, in real life situations, occlusion can occur anytime a subject passes behind an object with respect to a camera.

2.2.4   Clutter

Presence of background clutter makes the task of segmentation difficult. It is hard to model a background that reliably produces the clutter background and separates the moving foreground objects from that.

2.2.5   Camouflage

Intentionally or not, some objects may poorly differ from the appearance of background, making correct classification difficult. This is especially important in surveillance applications. Camouflage is particularly a problem for temporal differencing methods.

2.2.6   Presence of Shadows

Shadows cast by foreground objects often complicate further processing steps subsequent to background subtraction. Overlapping shadows of foreground regions for example hinder their separation and classification. Researchers have proposed different methods for detection of shadows.

2.2.7   Motion of the Camera

Video may be captured by unstable (e.g. vibrating) cameras. The jitter magnitude varies from one video to another.

2.2.8   Bootstrapping

If initialization data which is free from foreground objects is not available, the background model has to be initialized using a bootstrapping strategy.

2.2.9   Video Noise

Video signal is generally superimposed with noise. Background subtraction approaches for video surveillance have to cope with such degraded signals affected by different types of noise, such as sensor noise or compression artifacts.

2.2.10   Speed of the Moving Objects and Intermittent Object Motion

The speed of the moving object plays an important role in its detection. If the object is moving very slowly, the temporal differencing method will fail to detect the portions of the object preserving uniform region. On the other hand a very fast moving object leaves a trail of ghost region behind it in the detected foreground mask.

Intermittent motions of objects cause 'ghosting' artifacts in the detected motion, i.e., objects move, then stop for a short while, after which they start moving again. There may be situations when a video includes still objects that suddenly start moving, e.g., a parked vehicle driving away, and also abandoned objects.

2.2.11   Challenging Weather

Detection of moving object becomes a very difficult job when videos are captured in challenging weather conditions (winter weather conditions, i.e., snow storm, snow on the ground, fog), air turbulence etc.

2.3   Object Tracking

Object detection in videos involves verifying the presence of an object in a sequence of image frames. A very closely related topic in video processing is possibly the locating of objects for recognition – known as object tracking.

There are a wide variety of applications of object detecting and tracking in computer vision—video surveillance, vision-based control, video compression, human-computer interfaces, robotics etc. In addition, it provides input to higher level vision tasks, such as 3D reconstruction and representation. It also plays an important role in video databases such as content-based indexing and retrieval.

Popular methods of object tracking are summarized below.

2.3.1   Mean-shift

Mean-shift is an approach [12] to feature space analysis. This is an iterative approach which shifts a data point to the average of data points in its neighborhood similar to clustering. It has found its application in visual tracking [13, 14] and probability density estimation.

Mean Shift tracking uses fixed color distribution. In some applications, color distribution can change, e.g., due to rotation in depth. Continuous Adaptive Mean Shift (CAMSHIFT) [15]. CAMSHIFT can handle dynamically changing color distribution by adapting the search window size and computing color distribution in a search window.

2.3.2 KLT

The Kanade–Lucas–Tomasi (KLT) feature tracker is basically a feature extraction approach. It is based on the early work of Lucas and Kanade on an iterative image registration technique [16] that makes use of spatial intensity gradients to guide the search towards the best match. The method was developed fully by Tomasi and Kanade [17].

2.3.3 Condensation

A new approach the Condensation algorithm (Conditional Density Propagation) [18] which allows quite general representations of probability. Experimental results show that this increased generality does indeed lead to a marked improvement in tracking performance. In addition to permitting high-quality tracking in clutter, the simplicity of the Condensation algorithm also allows the use of non-linear motion models more complex than those commonly used in Kalman filters.

2.3.4 TLD

TLD [19] is an award-winning, real-time algorithm for tracking of unknown objects in video streams. The object of interest is defined by a bounding box in a single frame. TLD simultaneously tracks the object, learns its appearance and detects it whenever it appears in the video. The result is a real-time tracking that often improves over time. Tracking objects through highly cluttered scenes is difficult. Tracking becomes a challenging task under the following agile moving objects, in the presence of dense background clutter, probabilistic algorithms are essential. Algorithms based on Kalman filter, have been limited in the range of probability distributions they represent.

2.3.5 Tracking Based on Boundary of the Object

Boundary-based approaches are also referred to as edge-based approaches rely on the information provided by the object boundaries. It has been widely adopted in object tracking because the edges (boundary-based features) provide reliable information which is not dependent upon the motion type or the shape of the objects. Usually, the boundary-based tracking algorithms employ active contour models like snakes and geodesic active contours. These models are based on minimization of energy or geometric features by evolving an initial curve under the influence of external potentials, while being constrained by internal energies.

i. **Snakes:** Snakes introduced by Terzopoulos et al. [20] is a deformable active contour model used for boundary tracking. Snakes moves under the influence of image-intensity forces, subject to certain internal deformation constraints. In segmentation and boundary tracking problems, these forces relate to the gradient of image intensity and the positions of image features. One advantage of the force-driven snake model is that it can easily incorporate the dynamics derived from time-varying images. The snakes are usually parameterized and the solution space is constrained to have a predefined shape. So these methods require an accurate initialization step since the initial contour converges iteratively toward the solution of a partial differential equation. Considerable work has been done by several researchers to overcome the numerical problems associated with the solution of the equations of motion and to improve robustness in the presence of clutter and occlusions in the scenes.

ii. **Geodesic Active Contour Models:** These models are not parameterized and can be used to track objects that undergo non-rigid motion. Caselles et al. presented [21] a three step approach which start by detecting the contours of the objects to be tracked. An estimation of the velocity vector field along the detected contours is then performed. Subsequently, a partial differential equation is designed to move the contours to the boundary of the moving objects. These contours are then used as initial estimates of the contours in the next image and the process iterates.

Bibliography

1. A. M. McIvor; "Background subtraction techniques", Proc. of Image and Vision Computing, 2000.
2. J. Heikkila and O. Silven, "A real-time system for monitoring of cyclists and pedestrians", Proc. of 2nd IEEE Workshop on Visual Surveillance, pp. 74–81, 1999.
3. A. J. Lipton, H. Fujiyoshi, and R.S. Patil; "Moving target classification and tracking from real-time video", Proc. of Workshop Applications of Computer Vision, pp. 129–136, 1998.
4. L. Wang, W. Hu, and T. Tan; "Recent developments in human motion analysis", Pattern Recognition, Vol. 36 (3), pp. 585–601, 2003.
5. R. T. Collins et al. A system for video surveillance and monitoring: VSAM final report. Technical report CMU-RI-TR-00-12, Robotics Institute, Carnegie Mellon University, May 2000.
6. C. Stauffer, W. E. L. Grimson; "Adaptive background mixture models for real-time tracking", IEEE Int. Conf. on Computer Vision and Pattern Recognition (CVPR), Vol. 2, 1999.
7. I. Haritaoglu, D. Harwood, L. Davis; "W4: real-time surveillance of people and their activities", IEEE Transactions on Pattern Analysis and Machine Intelligence, Vol. 22 (8), pp. 809–830, 2000.
8. N. Paragios, R. Deriche; "Geodesic active contours and level sets for the detection and tracking of moving objects", IEEE Transactions on Pattern Analysis and Machine Intelligence, Vol. 22 (3), pp. 266–280, 2000.
9. L.Wixson, "Detecting Salient Motion by Accumulating Directionally-Consistent Flow", IEEE Transactions on Pattern Analysis and Machine Intelligence, Vol. 22 (8), 2000.

10. Robert Pless, Tomas Brodsky and Yiannis Aloimonos, "Detecting Independent Motion: The Statistics of Temporal Continuity", IEEE Transactions on Pattern Analysis and Machine Intelligence, Vol. 22 (8), 2000.
11. Gregory D. Hager and Peter N. Belhumeur; "Efficient Region Tracking With Parametric Models of Geometry and Illumination", IEEE Transactions on Pattern Analysis and Machine Intelligence, Vol. 20 (10), pp. 1025–1039, 1998.
12. Y. Cheng; "Mean shift, mode seeking, and clustering", IEEE Trans. on Pattern Analysis and Machine Intelligence, Vol. 17 (8), pp. 790–799, 1998.
13. D. Comaniciu, V. Ramesh, and P. Meer; "Real-time tracking of non-rigid objects using mean shift", IEEE Proc. on Computer Vision and Pattern Recognition, pp. 673–678, 2000.
14. D. Comaniciu, V. Ramesh, and P. Meer; "Mean shift: A robust approach towards feature space analysis", IEEE Trans. on Pattern Analysis and Machine Intelligence, Vol. 24 (5), pp. 603–619, 2002.
15. G. R. Bradski; "Computer vision face tracking for use in a perceptual user interface", Intel Technology Journal, 2nd Quarter, 1998.
16. Bruce D. Lucas and Takeo Kanade; "An Iterative Image Registration Technique with an Application to Stereo Vision", International Joint Conference on Artificial Intelligence, pp. 674–679, 1981.
17. Carlo Tomasi and Takeo Kanade; "Detection and Tracking of Point Features. Carnegie Mellon University Technical Report", CMU-CS-91-132, 1991.
18. Michael, Isard; D.Phil. Thesis; "Visual Motion Analysis by Probabilistic Propagation of Conditional Density", Oxford University, 1998.
19. Z. Kalal, K. Mikolajczyk, and J. Matas, "Tracking-Learning-Detection," Pattern Analysis and Machine Intelligence, 2011.
20. M. Kass, A. Witkin, and D. Terzopoulos, Snakes: Active Contour Models. Int'l J. Computer Vision, Vol. 1, pp. 321–332, 1988.
21. V. Caselles and B. Coll, Snakes in Movement. SIAM J. Numerical Analysis, Vol. 33, pp. 2, 445–2, 456, 1996.

Chapter 3
Moving Object Detection Using Background Subtraction

3.1 Background Subtraction

Background subtraction (shown in Fig. 3.1) is a widely used approach for detecting moving objects in videos from static cameras. The rationale in the approach is that of detecting the moving objects from the difference between the current frame and a reference frame, often called *background image*, or *background model*. Background subtraction is mostly done if the image in question is a part of a video stream.

A robust background subtraction algorithm should be able to handle lighting changes, repetitive motions from clutter and long-term scene changes. The following analyses make use of the function of $V(x,y,t)$ as a video sequence where t is the time dimension, x and y are the pixel spatial location variables, e.g. $V(1,2,3)$ represents the pixel intensity at spatial location $(1,2)$ of the image at $t = 3$ in the video sequence.

3.2 A Simple Background Subtraction Method using Frame Differencing

Frame difference (absolute) at time $t + 1$ is defined as

$$D(t+1) = \left| V(x, y, t+1) - V(x, y, t) \right|$$

The background is assumed to be the frame at time t. This difference image would only show some intensity for the pixel locations which have changed in the two frames. Seemingly the background is removed as in the ideal situation the difference between intensity levels for the background pixels is zero; however this approach will only work for cases where all foreground pixels are moving and all background pixels are static.

A threshold "Th" can be put on this difference image to improve the process of background subtraction.

S. H. Shaikh et al., *Moving Object Detection Using Background Subtraction*, SpringerBriefs in Computer Science, DOI 10.1007/978-3-319-07386-6_3, © The Author(s) 2014

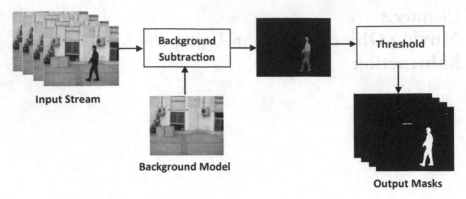

Fig. 3.1 Background subtraction. Source: Original frames from CASIA [33]

$$\left| V(x, y, t+1) - V(x, y, t) \right| > Th$$

This means that the pixel intensities of the difference image are thresholded or filtered on the basis of value of *Th*. The accuracy of this approach is dependent on speed of movement of the object in the scene. Faster movements may require higher thresholds.

3.3   A Brief Review of the Literature on Moving Object Detection

Over the years researchers have proposed a number of methodologies for modeling and subtraction background e.g. statistical methods [1–4], multilayer codebook-based method [5], methods for compressed streaming video [6], pixel intensity appearance profile based method [7], background subtraction in multi-sensor environments [8, 9] etc.

Piccardi presents a framework [10] for comparing a number of background subtraction techniques identifying the benefits and limitations of different methodologies. A review of a number of methods and an original categorization based on speed, memory requirements and accuracy are also reported in [10].

There are several problems related to the task of separating the foreground pixels from the background using background subtraction i.e. the presence of blurred boundaries between background and foreground objects. There are several open issues worth addressing under different points of view. In [9] a comprehensive review of the background subtraction methods is presented. Paper [9] also considers channels other than the sole visible optical one (such as the audio and the infrared channels). In addition, this paper discusses about novel approaches in particular, the multi-sensor direction seems to be well-suited to solve or simplify several background subtraction problems.

The method proposed by Stauffer et al. [1] focuses on motion tracking and shows how one can use observed motion to learn patterns of activity in a site. Motion segmentation is based on an adaptive background subtraction method where each pixel is modeled as a mixture of Gaussians. An online approximation is followed for updating the model. The Gaussian distributions are then evaluated to determine which are most likely to result from a background process. This yields a stable, real-time outdoor tracker that reliably deals with repetitive motions from clutter, lighting changes and long-term scene changes. While a tracking system is unaware of the identity of any object it tracks, the identity remains the same for the entire tracking sequence. The method leverages this information by accumulating joint co-occurrences of the representations within a sequence. These joint co-occurrence statistics are then used to create a hierarchical binary-tree classification of the representations. The method is useful for classifying sequences, as well as individual instances of activities in a site.

In [2] a mixture of Gaussian distributions has been used for modeling the pixel intensities, assuming that more than one process can be observed over time. Pixel values that do not fit the background distributions are considered as foreground.

The segmentation of moving regions can be achieved by combining results of background subtraction and temporal image analysis. Elhabian et al. present [11] a survey of moving object detection techniques in spatial domain using background removal.

Abbott et al. present [12] a method for decreasing computational cost in visual tracking systems by using track state estimates to direct and constrain image segmentation via background subtraction and connected components analysis.

Conventional background subtraction techniques that update an online background model have difficulties with correctly segmenting foreground objects if sudden brightness changes occur. Other methods that learn a global scene model offline suffer from projection errors. To overcome this, a method is presented in [13] using local and discriminative model for background subtraction. In this approach for each pixel a classifier is trained to decide whether the pixel belongs to the background or foreground. The paper claims that such a model requires significantly less tuning effort and exhibits better robustness.

Detecting moving objects by using an adaptive background model is a critical component for many vision-based applications. In [14] a method is proposed that combines pixel-based and block-based approaches into a single framework in building an efficient hierarchical background. In addition, a descriptor is proposed for block-based background modeling in the coarse level of the hierarchy.

Shadow detection is another interesting issue in the context of moving object detection. Leone et al. in [15] present a texture analysis-based approach for shadow detection of moving objects in visual surveillance environment, improving localization, segmentation, tracking and classification of detected objects. An automatic segmentation procedure based on adaptive background difference is performed in order to detect potential shadow points so that, for all moving pixels, the approach evaluates the compatibility of photometric properties with shadow characteristics. The shadow detection approach is improved by evaluating the similarity between little textured patches, since shadow regions present same textural characteristics in each frame and in the corresponding adaptive background model which is unaffected by scene type, background type or light conditions. The effectiveness of the method is verified using benchmark indoor and outdoor video sequences.

Background subtraction methods have been used to obtain human silhouettes for gesture and gait recognition. However, background subtraction in pixel units is prone to error which decreases recognition performance significantly. In [16] a background subtraction method is presented that extracts foreground objects in region units. Together with the background model, an object's color and movement information are used to obtain the effective region object likelihood. Then an adaptive region decision function determines the object regions.

Paper [17] presents a pixel-level background subtraction method using recursive equations that are used for updating the parameters of a Gaussian mixture model and to simultaneously select the appropriate number of components for each pixel. In the paper a simple non-parametric adaptive density estimation method is also presented for background subtraction.

Marko et al. present [18] a texture-based method for modeling the background and detecting moving objects from a video sequence. Each pixel is modeled as a group of adaptive local binary pattern histograms that are calculated over a circular region around the pixel. There are problems arising in the analysis of outdoor daylight scenes e.g. continuous variations of lighting conditions that cause unexpected changes in intensities on the background reference image makes the modeling of the background a difficult task. Paper [19] addresses this issue of illumination changes. In [19] a foreground segmentation algorithm is presented that combines temporal image analysis with a reference background image. In this method all the pixels in the image, even those covered by foreground objects, are continuously updated in the background model. The use of radiometric similarity between regions to compare pixels, both in the temporal image analysis and in the background subtraction has shown to solve the problems of small movement of vegetations, gradual variations of light conditions, and also ghost elimination when background objects moves in the scene.

In [20], three dynamic background subtraction algorithms for colour images are presented and compared. Using an invariant colour filter and a suitable motion tracking technique, an object-level classification is offered that recognizes the behaviours of all foreground blobs. This approach which selectively excludes foreground blobs from the background frame is included in all three methods. It is shown that the selective update using temporal median produces the correct background image for each input frame. One of the advantages of this algorithm is its ability to operate in unconstrained outdoor and indoor scenes. Also it is able to handle difficult situations such as removing ghosts and including stationary objects in the background image efficiently.

In [21], ratio images are considered as the basis for motion detection. The effects of illumination changes are smoothed out by the use of ratio images. The problem of the threshold selection, usually related to the difference image, is shifted onto the ratio image, even though an automatic procedure based on histograms is presented to address this. The superiority of motion detection based on ratio images is also depicted in experimentation.

An interesting approach is presented in [22] making use of spectral, spatial and temporal features, incorporated in a Bayesian framework, for characterizing the background appearance at each pixel. The method seems to work well in the presence of both static and dynamic backgrounds.

A background subtraction method is presented in [23] for the foreground detection from a non-stationary camera. Usually, motion compensation is required when applying background subtraction to a non-stationary background. In practice, it is difficult to realize this to sufficient pixel accuracy. The problem is further complicated when the moving objects to be detected/tracked are small, since the pixel error in motion compensating the background will hide the small targets. A spatial distribution of Gaussians model is presented in [23] to deal with moving object detection where the motion compensation is not exact but approximated. The distribution of each background pixel is temporally and spatially modeled. Based on this statistical model, a pixel in the current frame is classified as belonging to the foreground or background. In addition, a background restoration and adaptation algorithm is developed [23] for the non-stationary background over an extended period of time.

In [24], a general-purpose method has been proposed that combines statistical assumptions with the object-level knowledge of moving objects, apparent objects (ghosts), and shadows acquired in the processing of the previous frames. Pixels belonging to moving objects, ghosts, and shadows are processed differently in order to supply an object-based selective update. The proposed approach exploits color information for both background subtraction and shadow detection to improve object segmentation and background update. The approach is proven to be fast, flexible, and precise in terms of both pixel accuracy and reactivity to background changes.

Intensity is expressed as the multiplication of illumination and reflectance, the logarithmic intensity is therefore the addition of logarithmic illumination and logarithmic reflectance, which are easier to be separated and analyzed than the multiplication of illumination and reflectance. This idea has been exploited by Wu et al. in [25] towards a simple background subtraction method based on logarithmic intensities of pixels. The method achieves results superior to traditional difference algorithms making the problem of threshold selection less critical.

In [26] color and edge information have been used both for background modeling and for subtraction, using confidence maps to fuse intermediate results. These approaches work well with slight illumination changes, but cannot often handle either large, sudden changes in the scene or multiple moving objects in the scene.

In [27] a real time visual surveillance system (W4) is presented for detecting and tracking multiple people and monitoring their activities in an outdoor environment. W4 employs a combination of shape analysis and tracking to locate people and their parts (head, hands, feet, torso) and to create models of people's appearance so that they can be tracked through interactions such as occlusions. It can determine whether a foreground region contains multiple people and can segment the region into its constituent people and track them. It can also determine whether people are carrying objects, and can segment objects from their silhouettes, and construct appearance models for them so they can be identified in subsequent frames. W4 can recognize events between people and objects, such as depositing an object, exchanging bags, or removing an object.

A non-parametric background modeling technique is introduced in [28]. It estimates the probability of observing a pixel intensity value based on a sample of intensity values for each pixel. The algorithm works well with small movements of vegetation, and uses color information to suppress shadows of the targets.

Due to the noise in the image, the results can be unreliable if a simple threshold process is used. Therefore, many background subtraction algorithms have introduced noise measurements to extract moving objects. A review of some of the techniques for background subtraction is presented in [29].

Handling dynamic background conditions in a scene has been one of the challenging tasks in moving object detection from video. A method is presented in [4] for dealing with dynamic background scenes. It presents an adaptive model for backgrounds containing significant stochastic motion (e.g. water). The model is based on a generalization of the Stauffer-Grimson background model, where each mixture component is modeled as a dynamic texture. An online K-means algorithm is used for updating the parameters using a set of sufficient statistics of the model.

A multilayer codebook-based background subtraction model is reported in [5] for video sequences to detect moving objects. Combination of multilayer block-based strategy and adaptive feature extraction from blocks of various sizes is considered. The method can remove most of the dynamic background and significantly increase the processing efficiency. Moreover, the pixel-based classification is adopted for refining the results from the block-based background subtraction, which can further classify pixels as foreground, shadows, and highlights. Researchers have also proposed background subtraction method [6] for surveillance applications in bitstreams encoded in the baseline profile of H.264/AVC.

In [7] a method is presented to model background considering the similarity in the intensity changes among pixels. Pixels are classified into several clusters based on the similarity of their intensity changes. Then by cluster analysis it is identified whether the significant intensity changes are caused by foreground objects or illumination changes.

In the recent years, the computer vision community has shown great interest on depth-based applications by virtue of new generation of RGB-D imagery. In [8] a background subtraction algorithm is presented based on the fusion of multiple region-based classifiers that processes depth and color data provided by RGB-D cameras. Foreground objects are detected by combining a region-based foreground prediction (based on depth data) with different background models (based on a Mixture of Gaussian algorithm) providing color and depth descriptions of the scene at pixel and region level. The information given by these modules is fused in a mixture to improve the foreground detection accuracy.

A background subtraction method that can work under complex environments is presented in [30]. The method consists of two stages: coarse foreground detection through the phase-based background model and foreground refinement using the distance transform. The background model is built where each pixel is modeled as a group of adaptive phase features. Although the foreground detection result produced by the background model only contains some sparse pixels, the basic structure of the foreground is captured as a whole. Finally a distance transform is adopted to aggregate the pixels surrounding the foreground so that the final result is more clear and integrated. The method can handle many complex situations including dynamic background and illumination variations, especially for sudden illumination change. In addition to this the method does not incorporate any background initialization constraints.

Hofmann et al. in [3] present a Pixel-Based Adaptive Segmenter (PBAS) method for foreground segmentation. It follows a nonparametric background modeling paradigm. The background is modeled by a history of recently observed pixel values. The foreground detection depends on a decision threshold. The background update is based on a learning parameter.

In [31] Hamad et al. present a method to detect and extract silhouettes of foreground objects from a video sequence of a static camera based on analyzing statistically the pixel history as time series observations. Motion detection is obtained by kernel density estimation. Two consecutive stages of the k-means clustering algorithm are utilized to identify the most reliable background regions and decrease the detection of false positives. Pixel and object based updating mechanism for the background model is presented to cope with challenges like gradual and sudden illumination changes, ghost appearance, non-stationary background objects, and moving objects that remain stable for more than the half of the training period.

Paper [32] presents a Fuzzy C-Means (FCM) algorithm to produce an adaptive threshold for background subtraction in moving object detection. To evaluate the performance, FCM is compared against standard Otsu's algorithm for threshold selection strategy. Mean Square Error (MSE) and Peak Signal Noise Ratio (PSNR) is used to measure the performance. FCM shows promising results in classifying the pixels as foreground or background in moving object detection.

Evaluation of different methods is necessary for comparative performance analysis. In [29] a set of background subtraction methods are evaluated on the basis of accuracy and time and space requirements.

There are a number of existing methodologies for background subtraction towards moving object detection. However, most of the methods are not suitable to be used for applications in resource constrained environments due to high computational complexity and storage requirements. A low-cost moving object detection technique is presented in Chap. 4 towards a possible solution to the existing problem.

Bibliography

1. C. Stauffer, W. E. L. Grimson; "Learning patterns of activity using real-time tracking", IEEE Transactions on Pattern Analysis and Machine Intelligence, Vol. 22 (8), pp. 747–757, 2000.
2. C. Stauffer, W. E. L. Grimson; "Adaptive background mixture models for real-time tracking", IEEE Int. Conf. on Computer Vision and Pattern Recognition (CVPR), Vol. 2, 1999.

3. M. Hofmann, P.Tiefenbacher, G. Rigoll; "Background Segmentation with Feedback: The Pixel-Based Adaptive Segmenter", IEEE Workshop on Change Detection, pp. 38–43, 2012.
4. A. B. Chan, V. Mahadevan, N. Vasconcelos; "Generalized Stauffer–Grimson background subtraction for dynamic scenes", Springer Journal on Machine Vision and Applications, Vol. 22 (5), pp. 751–766, 2011.
5. J.-M. Guo, C.-H. Hsia, Y.-F. Liu, M.-H. Shih, C.-H. Chang, J.-Y. Wu, "Fast Background Subtraction Based on a Multilayer Codebook Model for Moving Object Detection", IEEE Transactions on Circuits and Systems for Video Technology, Vol. 23 (10), pp. 1809–1821, 2013.
6. B. Dey, M.K. Kundu; "Robust Background Subtraction for Network Surveillance in H.264 Streaming Video", IEEE Transactions on Circuits and Systems for Video Technology, Vol. 23 (10), pp. 1695–1703, 2013.
7. S. Yoshinaga, A. Shimada, H. Nagahara, Rin-ichiro Taniguchi; "Background Model Based on Intensity Change Similarity Among Pixels", 19th Japan-Korea Joint Workshop on Frontiers of Computer Vision, pp. 276–280, 2013.
8. M. Camplani, C.R. Blanco, L. Salgado, F. Jaureguizar, N. Garcia; "Multi-sensor background subtraction by fusing multiple region-based probabilistic classifiers", Pattern Recognition Letters, Available online 4 October 2013, ISSN 0167-8655, doi:http://dx.doi.org/10.1016/j.patrec.2013.09.022.
9. M. Cristani, M. Farenzena, D. Bloisi, V. Murino; "Background subtraction for automated multisensor surveillance: a comprehensive review", EURASIP Journal on Advances in Signal Processing, Vol. 2010 (43), pp. 1–24, 2010.
10. M. Piccardi; "Background subtraction techniques : A review", IEEE Int. Conf on Systems, Man and Cybernetics (SMC), Vol. 4, pp. 3199–3104, 2004.
11. S. Elhabian, K. El-Sayed, S. Ahmed; "Moving object detection in spatial domain using background removal techniques—State-of-Art", Recent Patents on Computer Science, Vol. 1, pp. 32–54, 2008.
12. R.G. Abbott, L.R. Williams; "Multiple target tracking with lazy background subtraction and connected components analysis", Springer Journal on Machine Vision and Applications, Vol. 20 (2), pp. 93–101, 2009.
13. A. Ulges, T.M. Breuel; "A Local Discriminative Model for Background Subtraction", Proceedings of 30th DAGM Symposium, pp. 507–516, 2008.
14. Y. T. Chen, C.S. Chen, C.R. Huang, Y.P. Hung; "Efficient hierarchical method for background subtraction", Pattern Recognition, Vol. 40 (10), pp. 2706–2715, 2007.
15. A. Leone, C. Distante; "Shadow detection for moving objects based on texture analysis", Pattern Recognition, Vol. 40 (4), pp. 1222–1233, 2007.
16. J.H. Ahn, H. Byun, "Human Silhouette Extraction Method Using Region Based Background Subtraction", Proc. 3rd Int., MIRAGE, pp. 412–420, 2007.
17. Z. Zivkovic, F. van der Heijden; "Efficient adaptive density estimation per image pixel for the task of background subtraction", Pattern Recognition Letters, Vol. 27 (7), pp. 773–780, 2006.
18. H. Marko, P. Matti; "A Texture-Based Method for Modeling the Background and Detecting Moving Objects", IEEE Transactions on Pattern Analysis and Machine Intelligence, Vol. 28 (4), pp. 657–662, 2006.
19. P. Spagnolo, T.D' Orazio, M. Leo, A. Distante; "Moving object segmentation by background subtraction and temporal analysis", Image and Vision Computing, Vol. 24 (5), pp. 411–423, 2006.
20. B. Shoushtarian, H. E. Bez; "A practical adaptive approach for dynamic background subtraction using an invariant colour model and object tracking", Pattern Recognition Letters, Vol. 26 (1), pp. 5–26, 2005.
21. Q.Z. Wu, H.Y. Cheng, B.S. Jeng; "Motion detection via change-point detection for cumulative histograms of ratio images", Pattern Recognition Letters, Vol. 26 (5), pp. 555–563, 2005.
22. L. Li, W. Huang, I.Y.H. Gu, Q. Tian; "Statistical modeling of complex backgrounds for foreground object detection", IEEE Transactions on Image Processing, Vol. 13 (11), pp. 1459–1472, 2004.

23. Y. Ren, C.S Chua, Y.K. Ho; "Statistical background modeling for non-stationary camera", Pattern Recognition Letters, Vol. 24 (1–3), pp. 183–196, 2003.

24. R. Cucchiara, C. Grana, M. Piccardi, A. Prati; "Detecting moving objects, ghosts, and shadows in video streams", IEEE Transactions on Pattern Analysis and Machine Intelligence, Vol. 25 (10), pp. 1337–1342, 2003.

25. Q.Z. Wu, B. S. Jeng; "Background subtraction based on logarithmic intensities", Pattern Recognition Letters, Vol. 23 (13), pp. 1529–1536, 2002.

26. S. Jabri, Z. Duric, H. Wechsler, A. Rosenfeld; "Detection and location of people in video images using adaptive fusion of colour and edge information", Proc. 15th Int. Conf. on Pattern Recognition, Vol. 4, pp. 627–630, 2000.

27. I. Haritaoglu, D. Harwood, L. Davis; "W4: real-time surveillance of people and their activities", IEEE Transactions on Pattern Analysis and Machine Intelligence, Vol. 22 (8), pp. 809–830, 2000.

28. A. Elgammal, D. Harwood, L. Davis; "Non-parametric model for background subtraction", IEEE Frame Rate Workshop, pp. 751–767, 2000.

29. H. Hassanpour, M. Sedighi, A. Manashty; "Video Frame's Background Modeling : Reviewing the Techniques", Journal of Signal and Information Processing, Vol. 2 (2), pp. 72–78, 2011.

30. X. Gengjian, S. Jun, S. Li, "Background subtraction based on phase feature and distance transform", Pattern Recognition Letters, Vol. 33 (12), pp. 1601–1613, 2012.

31. A. M. Hamad, N. Tsumura; "Background subtraction based on time-series clustering and statistical modeling", Optical Review. Vol. 19 (2), pp. 110–120, 2012.

32. M.A. Soeleman, M.Hariadi, M.H.Purnomo; "Adaptive threshold for background subtraction in moving object detection using Fuzzy C-Means clustering", IEEE Region 10 Conference TENCON, pp. 1–5, 2012.

33. L. Wang, T. Tieniu, N. Huazhong, H. Weiming; "Silhouette analysis-based gait recognition for human identification", IEEE Transactions on Pattern Analysis and Machine Intelligence Vol. 25, pp. 1505–1518, 2003.

Chapter 4
Moving Object Detection: A New Approach

This chapter presents a novel background subtraction technique for detecting moving objects from video under dynamic background conditions. The presented methodology is a simple and low-cost solution for modeling and updating background during a background subtraction process. Comparative performance analysis with other state-of-the-art methods on benchmark data-set shows the effectiveness of the proposed method. The objective of the research is not to claim that the proposed method yields the best result in terms of accuracy; rather the main novelty is in its low computational cost. However, in spite of being less computation-intensive, comparative analysis reveals that the new method produces quite competitive results as compared to other methods. The proposed method would be useful particularly for applications in resource constrained environments by virtue of its low computation time and storage requirements.

4.1 Introduction

Background subtraction is a widely used approach towards detecting moving objects in videos. The approach consists of two steps: modeling and updating of a background frame and performing subtraction between the current image and the background model. As a basis, a background image needs to represent the scene with no moving objects and it must regularly be updated so as to adapt to the varying illumination conditions and geometric settings of the scene. Several methods for background subtraction have been proposed in the recent literature. These methods essentially aim to estimate the background model from the temporal sequence of the frames.

Reliable detection of moving objects from video is an important requirement for many computer vision-based systems. Motion detection can be used to determine the presence of people, vehicles or other unexpected objects in video surveillance applications. This is the first step in most of the surveillance systems followed by more complex activity recognition steps. Background subtraction methods are widely exploited for moving object detection in videos in many applications, such as traffic monitoring, human motion capture, and video surveillance.

S. H. Shaikh et al., *Moving Object Detection Using Background Subtraction,*   25
SpringerBriefs in Computer Science, DOI 10.1007/978-3-319-07386-6_4,
© The Author(s) 2014

4.2   Motivation of the Work

A number of limitations of existing background subtraction techniques are evident from the review work as documented in Chap. 3. A background that is modeled considering initial frame sequence of a video (supposing that these frames do not contain any moving object so good for modeling an ideal background) suffers from reflecting recent changes in the scene like illumination changes. If only recent frames are considered for generating the background, it is often found that some unwanted regions appear in the foreground in the form of a ghost region [1].

One of the challenging tasks is the detection of foreground moving objects in the presence of dynamic backgrounds [2]. Misdetection becomes obvious when the background contains moving elements in the form of swaying tree branches, slight movements of tree leaves, presence of shimmering water or fountain etc. There are techniques that deal with dynamic background in the scene [3, 4]. However, the complex and time consuming process of modeling the background as well as updating the background makes them prohibitive for practical online applications.

In this context, this chapter presents a novel but simple background subtraction technique for dynamic scenes. It is low cost in terms of computational complexity. This would open up the scope of its usage for many interesting applications. It is particularly suitable for online detection of moving objects in embedded devices limited by less computation power and low preinstalled memory.

The rest of this chapter is organized as follows: Sect. 4.3 presents a new method of background subtraction, Sect. 4.4 describes different quantitative evaluation measures. Section 4.5 talks about the experimental dataset; the performance of the proposed method is analyzed in the experimental verification section in 4.6, where the results of the proposed method with respect to ground-truths are given. In the same section a quantitative performance analysis is presented for comparing the proposed method with others [4–6]. Section 4.7 briefly explains the reasons of low-cost computational and storage requirements of the method. Comparative analysis of time and space complexity of the proposed method along with others is presented in Sect. 4.8. Section 4.9 describes the usefulness of the method for a surveillance application.

4.3   A New Method of Background Subtraction

The new method is a background subtraction technique for detecting moving objects under dynamic background conditions. One of the major benefits of this method is that all the processing is done using gray-scale frames. A color frame is to be converted to gray scale and processed further. This is especially suited for applications which require online transmission of the video. Transmission of a gray-scale video saves huge bandwidth and time compared to transmitting a color video.

The proposed methodology consists of the following major processing steps: modeling background, block processing, background update, background subtraction and post-processing.

i.   *Modeling Background:* A background model is generated by considering the *median* of corresponding pixels of previous *n* frames.Background modeling is done using *median* of grayscale intensities of each corresponding pixel on last *k* frames. Background frame at time *t* for a particular pixel *x* (denoted as x_t) is calculated as follows:

$$BG(x_t) = median\{x_i \mid i = m_1 \text{ to } m_2\} \text{ where } m_1$$
$$= t - k - bg\_offset \text{ and } m_2 = t - bg\_offset$$

The value of *k* depends on the type of video being processed. The idea is to keep the value of *k* sufficiently large so as to model a realistic background at the same time reflecting the recent background changes. If frames that came long ago in the sequence (compared to the present frame) are considered in the background modeling, this will not be able to reflect recent changes in the scene. On the contrary, if only recent frames are considered for background generation, the recent changes will be reflected in the scene which sometimes would generate erroneous detected foreground pixels (e.g. unwanted effects like ghost regions) after background subtraction. Therefore, in this approach a total of *k* number of frames is considered for background modeling. If the index of the present frame is *t*, frames starting from $t - k - bg\_offset$ to $t - bg\_offset$ are considered for modeling the background. The value of the parameters *k* and *bg_offset* accounts for a balance between incorporating recent changes in the scene and the attributes that change slowly in the background of the scene.

ii.   *Block Processing:* The present frame and the modeled background are divided into a number of logical blocks B_{ij}. Each block in the present frame is compared with the corresponding block in the background on the basis of a similarity measure. Similarity is computed using 2D correlation coefficient. Similarity coefficient (*sim_coff*) is computed for each block B_{ij}. Let *A* represent a block in the present frame and *B* be the corresponding block in the background frame. Let $\bar{A}$ and $\bar{B}$ represent the mean of a block for the present and the background frames, respectively. The dimension of each logical block is assumed to be *mxn*.

The block similarity coefficient is defined as follows:

$$sim - coff = \frac{\sum_m \cdot \sum_n (A_{mn} - \bar{A})(B_{mn} - \bar{B})}{\sqrt{\sum_m \cdot \sum_n (A_{mn} - \bar{A})^2 \sum_m \cdot \sum_n (B_{mn} - \bar{B})^2}}$$

Scene change is detected for a block B_{ij} if $sim\_coff\ (B_{ij}) < Th_{BS}$ and a foreground mask is generated for that block. All other blocks are considered to have not changed, so they are marked and not processed in further steps.

Block processing generates a binary mask ($F_{Mask_{BP}}$) containing all the sub-blocks B_{ij} for which the similarity coefficient is less than the threshold Th_{BS}.

$$F_{Mask_{BP}} = 1, \text{ if } sim\_coff\ (B_{ij}) < Th_{BS}.$$
$$= 0, \text{ otherwise.}$$

The value of Th_{BS} is kept in the range from 0.3 to 0.5.

This step significantly reduces computational load as a large portion of the current frame is discarded from further processing in subsequent steps.

iii. *Background Update:* It is important to keep the background updated for subsequent background subtraction steps. During block processing, each frame is subdivided into several smaller logical blocks and change detection is done by computing the similarity coefficient and comparing each block in the current frame with the corresponding block in the background frame. A *block_change* parameter is computed. It represents the percentage of blocks that are marked changed during the block processing step with respect to the total number of blocks present in a frame.

$$block\_change = \frac{number\_of\_changed\_blocks}{total\_number\_of\_blocks} x100$$

A parameter known as frame threshold Th_{Frm} is set which works as a decision parameter for background updating. If the difference of *block_change* parameters for two consecutive frames is less than Th_{Frm}, the background is not updated for the next frame in the sequence and background subtraction is continued considering the previously modeled background.

iv. *Background Subtraction:* All the blocks selected as *changed* in the previous step are further analyzed for computing pixel statistics e.g. *mean*, standard deviation (*sd*), minimum (*min*) and maximum (*max*) of intensity values. Previous b frames in the temporal sequence with respect to the present frame are considered for computing the pixel statistics.

The block statistics vector for each block B_{ij} is calculated as follows

$$B_{Stat}\left(B_{ij}\right) = \left[V_{mean_{ij}}, V_{sd_{ij}}, V_{min_{ij}}, V_{max_{ij}}\right]$$
$$\forall B_{ij} \epsilon F_{Mask_{BP}}$$

$v_{mean}(x_i) = mean\ (x_i^{t-b}, x_i^{t-b+1}, \ldots\ldots\ x_i^{t-1})$ is the mean of intensity values of the pixel x_i in past b number of temporal frames from $t-b$ to $t-1$. Here t represents the temporal sequence number of the current frame; and $V_{mean_{ij}} = \{v_{mean}(x_k)\ |\ \forall k = 1, 2, \ldots. m*n\}$.

Similarly, the standard deviation, minimum and maximum of intensity values of the pixel x_i for past b temporal frames are calculated as follows:

$$v_{sd}(x_i) = sd(x_i^{t-b}, x_i^{t-b+1}, \ldots x_i^{t-1})$$
$$v_{min}(x_i) = min(x_i^{t-b}, x_i^{t-b+1}, \ldots x_i^{t-1})$$
$$v_{max}(x_i) = max(x_i^{t-b}, x_i^{t-b+1}, \ldots x_i^{t-1})$$

Moreover, the following vectors are generated

$$V_{sd_{ij}} = \{v_{sd}(x_k) \mid \forall k = 1, 2, \ldots m * n\}$$
$$V_{min_{ij}} = \{v_{min}(x_k) \mid \forall k = 1, 2, \ldots m * n\}$$
$$V_{max_{ij}} = \{v_{max}(x_k) \mid \forall k = 1, 2, \ldots m * n\}$$

The value of b is an important parameter as pixel statistics generally reflect recent change in the scene. If the value of b is very large, recent changes will not be accumulated in the statistics. The value of b is kept between 10 and 20. The exact value depends on the type of video being processed. Subsequently, all the pixels lying in a connected block are considered for background subtraction. A tuning parameter p is set in the range $0.5 \leq p \leq 0.8$ for computing two pixel-level thresholds as follows:

$$Th(x_k)_{max} = V_{mean}(x_k) + V_{sd}(x_k) * p \text{ and}$$
$$Th(x_k)_{min} = V_{mean}(x_k) - V_{sd}(x_k) * p$$

Background subtraction is performed as follows:

$$F_{Mask}(x_k) = 1, \text{ if } \left(((x_k^t < Th_{min}(x_k)) \text{ OR } (x_k^t > Th_{min}(x_k)))\right)$$
$$\forall x_k \epsilon B_{ij} \epsilon F_{Mask_{BP}} \quad \text{ OR } \quad ((x_k^t < V_{min}(x_k)) \text{ OR } (x_k^t > V_{max}(x_k)))$$
$$= 0, \text{ otherwise.}$$

Here V_{min} and V_{max} represent the minimum and maximum vectors of the corresponding block $B_{ij}.x_k^t$ represents the intensity value of pixel x_k at current frame t.

v. *Post Processing:* Post processing is done on the foreground mask for noise reduction. In this step the blob extraction is done for identifying scattered foreground regions in the detected foreground mask. Moreover, the foreground mask is corrected by suppressing the connected regions that are very small in size.

Figure 4.1 shows the result on a sample frame from sequence Canoe of CDW12 [2] dataset. Figure 5.1 (b) is the present frame; (a) is the background computed using the method mentioned above; (c) is the output foreground regions detected by the proposed method.

Fig. 4.1 Results. (**a**) Background (**b**) Present Frame (**c**) Result

4.4   Evaluation Measures

Different evaluation measures have been suggested by the researchers [2]. The measures are defined in this section. The evaluation measures are based on the following parameters: **TP**=number of true positives; number of foreground pixels correctly detected as foreground. **TN**=number of true negatives; number of background pixels correctly detected as background. **FP**=number of false positives; number of pixels which are actually background but mistakenly detected as foreground and **FN**=number of false negatives; number of pixels which are actually foreground but mistakenly detected as background.

Recall: Recall is defined as the ratio of true positive to true positive and false negative.

$$\text{Re } call = \frac{TP}{TP + FN}$$

High value of recall is desired.

Specificity: Specificity is defined as the ratio of true negative to true negative and false positive.

$$Specificity = \frac{TN}{TN + FP}$$

False Positive Rate (FPR): FPR is the ratio of false positive to false positive and true negative. A lower score of this metric is desired.

$$FPR = \frac{FP}{FP + TN}$$

False Negative Rate (FNR): FNR is the ratio of false negative to true negative and false positive. As this is a metric representing falsely detected pixels so a lower score is better.

$$FNR = \frac{FN}{TN + FP}$$

Percentage of Wrong Classification (PWC): PWC is the ratio of false positive and false negative to all the detected pixels. A lower score for PWC stands for a better result.

$$PWC = \frac{FP + FN}{TP + FN + FP + TN} x100$$

Precision: Precision is the measure of how correctly the foreground is detected. It is the ratio of true positive to true positive and false positive.

$$\Pr ecision = \frac{TP}{TP + FP}$$

F-measure: In F-measure both recall and precision are integrated. A higher value for F-measure will represent a better score.

$$F - measure = \frac{2 * \operatorname{Re} call * \Pr ecision}{\operatorname{Re} call + \Pr ecision}$$

4.5 Experimental Dataset

The change detection benchmark dataset CDW12 [2] is used for performance analysis of the proposed method. There are six videos in this database in "*dynamic background*" category depicting outdoor scenes with strong (parasitic) background motions. Two videos represent boats on shimmering water (Boats, Canoe), two videos show cars passing next to a fountain (Fountain01, Fountain02), and two videos depict pedestrians, cars and trucks passing in front of a tree shaken by the wind (Fall, Overpass).

4.6 Experimental Verification

This section is divided into two subsections. In Sect. 4.6.1 the performance of the proposed method is analyzed based on the metrics defined in Sect. 4.5 on the basis of the ground-truth images provided in the dataset [2]. Section 4.6.2 presents the comparison of the proposed method with some of the others.

4.6.1 Performance Analysis of the Proposed Method

Table 4.1 collects the average results of the proposed method for all the seven evaluation measures defined in Sect. 4.4. Results are produced for all six benchmark videos of CDW12 [2] under dynamic background category.

The results in Table 4.1 show that for sequence Boats and Canoe more than 90 % Recall and 99 % Specificity scores are obtained. The score of F-measure for

Table 4.1 Average performance on all test sequences

Test Sequence	Recall	Specificity	FPR	FNR	PWC	Precision	F-Measure
BOATS	0.9140	0.9918	0.8237	0.4002	1.1695	0.8378	0.8742
CANOE	0.9277	0.9919	0.8095	0.5740	1.2817	0.9010	0.9142
FOUNTAIN01	0.8356	0.9994	0.0591	0.0479	0.1067	0.8044	0.8197
FOUNTAIN02	0.7575	0.9991	0.0947	0.1690	0.2619	0.8478	0.8742
FALL	0.6547	0.9924	0.7634	1.8117	2.4468	0.8182	0.7273
OVERPASS	0.7885	0.9905	0.9484	2.4473	3.0435	0.9058	0.8432

Canoe is also more than 90%. The number of false detection is significantly low for sequences Founiatn01 and Fountain02 as shown by the PWC scores. Very high scores of Specificity measure are also obtained for sequences Fall and Overpass. Figure 4.2 depicts the original color frames for each of the six videos along with the ground-truth frames and the outputs of the proposed method.

4.6.2 Comparison with Other Methods

The comparative performance analysis is performed considering three methods for moving object detection. The classic algorithm incorporating Gaussian Mixture Model (GMM) proposed by Stauffer and Grimson [4]; two recent methods—one proposed by Hoffman et al. [5] (Pixel-based Adaptive Segmenter, PBAS) and the pixel appearance profile-based spatio-temporal method (KDE) proposed by Yoshinaga et al. [6] are also considered.

Figure 4.3 shows the comparative results on the Boats sequence. As shown in the plot, the proposed method produces very competitive results. For measures like recall, specificity, precision and f-measure it stands hand to hand with others. False detection is high as suggested by metrics FPR and FNR. However, comparing results of other methods it is seen that the proposed method stands second for FPR after PBAS and for FNR after KDE.

Figure 4.4 shows comparative average performance of the proposed method with other three [4–6] on the sequence Canoe. As shown in the plot, for this sequence, the proposed method gives very competitive results for the measures like recall, specificity, precision and f-measure. However, FPR is highest for this method. It is also seen that FNR is comparatively low. For PWC measure the proposed method stands second after KDE.

Figure 4.5 shows comparative performance analysis for sequence Fountain01. As shown in the plot, the proposed method gives the best results for precision and F-measure. It also produces the lowest score for FPR and PWC suggesting that its performance is the best as far as the false detection is concerned. So, it more suitably handles the background dynamics imposed by the fountain in the scene. For other measures like recall and specificity it produces very competitive results.

Figure 4.6 shows the results of the proposed method along with other three for sequences Boats, Canoe and Fall. As shown by the results for the sequence Boats all the methods give almost similar performances. However, for Canoe it is seen

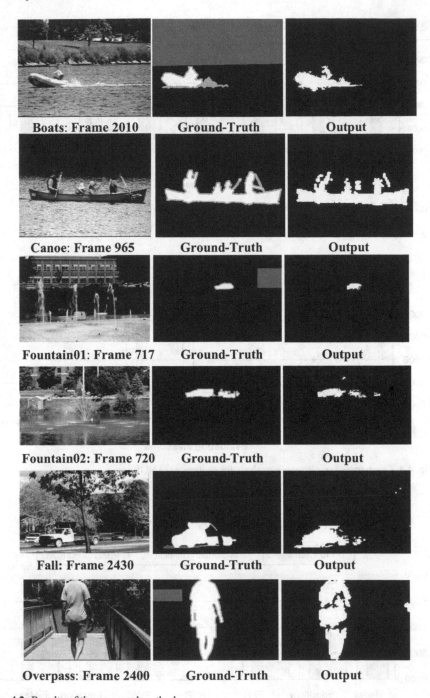

Fig. 4.2 Results of the proposed method

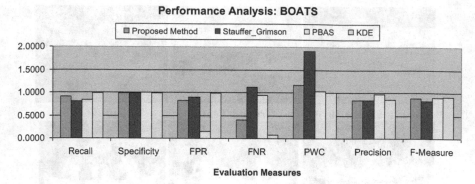

Fig. 4.3 Comparative performance analysis for sequence BOATS

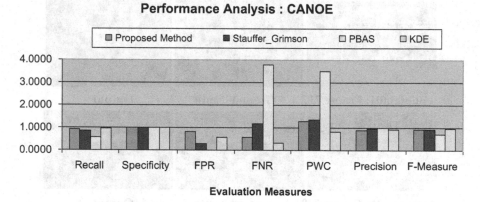

Fig. 4.4 Comparative performance analysis for sequence CANOE

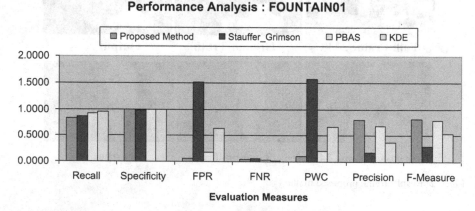

Fig. 4.5 Comparative performance analysis for sequence FOUNTAIN01

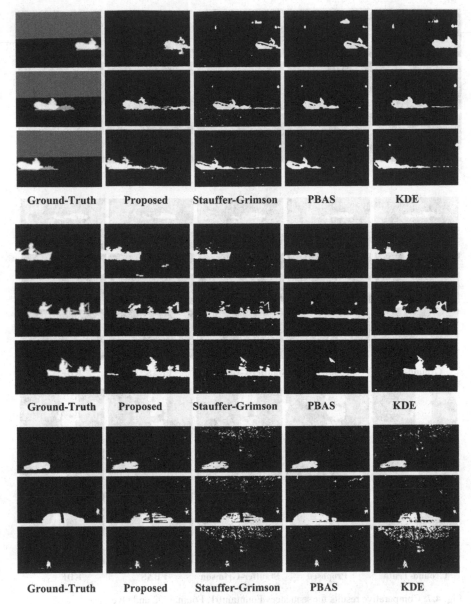

Fig. 4.6 Comparative results for sequences Boats, Canoe and Fall

that in terms of completeness of the shapes of the objects, KDE performs very good followed by the proposed method. PBAS miserably fails to detect the foreground regions as suggested by the output frames. In the results for sequence Fall, it is seen that Stauffer-Grimson fails to detect the motion of the tree branches, This is also true for KDE. Performance of PBAS is better. However the proposed method performs the best as far as the misdetection of background dynamics is concerned.

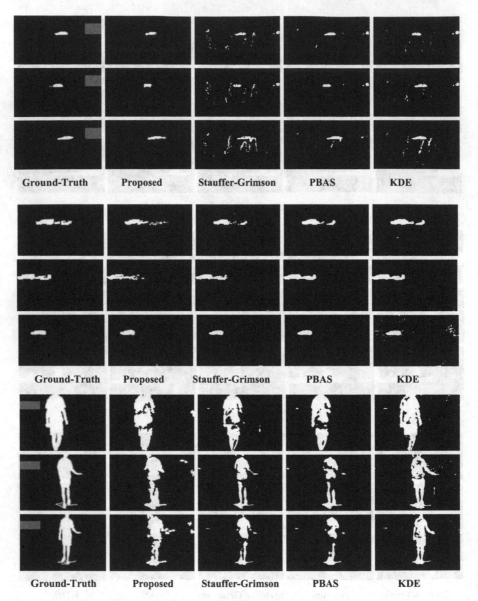

Fig. 4.7 Comparative results for sequences Fountain01, Fountain02 and Overpass

Figure 4.7 shows the similar results for sequences Fountain01, Fountain02 and Overpass. As shown by the results for the sequence Fountain01 the proposed method performs the best as it almost does not contain any false detection due to background dynamics. This is followed by PBAS and KDE. However, Stauffer-Grimson wrongly detects significant portions of the fountain as foreground.

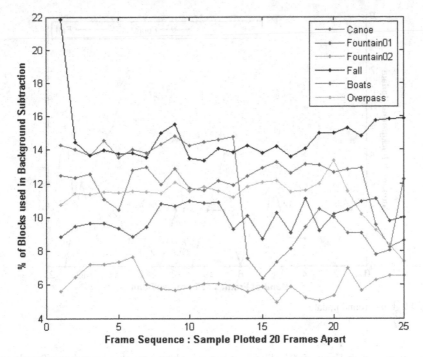

Fig. 4.8 Effect of block processing

The proposed method generates very competitive results for the sequence Fountain02. The performance of the proposed method is not so good for sequence Overpass. It falsely detects the regions of tree movements. However, as can be seen from the results of Stauffer-Grimson and PBAS, significant portions of the human body (region of legs) are discarded. KDE performs well for this sequence.

4.7   Effectiveness in Terms of Computation

Effect of Block Processing Block processing significantly reduces the number of pixels that actually participate in the background subtraction step. This has been proved experimentally as shown in Fig. 4.8.

A sequence of 500 frames is considered for each of six test videos. The number of blocks (percentage) marked as *changed* during block processing for each of these 500 frames is calculated. The statistics for each video is shown in separate color. The Y-axis shows the percentage of blocks (among all the blocks a frame is divided into) that participates in the background subtraction step for a particular frame. The X-axis represents the sequence of frames; for the sake of better representation, samples that are 20 frames apart are taken. For example, the blue line shows that

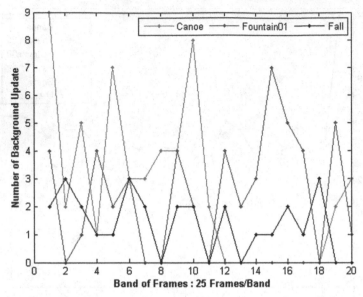

Fig. 4.9 Background update

plot for sequence Fountain01. The first sample shows a value just above 8 indicating the percentage of blocks that qualify as changed for that particular frame during
block processing. All other blocks for that frame are not processed in subsequent
steps. Similarly the first sample denoted by the red line represents that only 14 %
blocks qualify as changed during block processing for sequence Canoe.

This experiment shows that the actual number of blocks that participate in the
background subtraction process is significantly less than the total number of blocks
present in a frame.

Background Update Number of times the background is modeled or updated is
an important factor for a background subtraction technique. In the proposed method
the background is modeled by taking the median of a certain band of frames in the
sequence. A study has been made to analyze how many times the background is
generated by the proposed method for a sequence of 500 frames. Figure 4.9 shows
the results for three of the test videos.

The samples are given for a band of frames where each band contains 25 frames.
As for example, in Fig. 4.9 for the video Canoe, the first sample shown by the red
line is 9 for the first band indicating that in the sequence of the first 25 frames, the
background is generated only 9 times. In the next band this quantity is 2 indicating
that during processing of temporal sequence of frames from 26 to 50, the background is updated twice. In case of Fountain01, the first sample is 4 indicating
the number of background updates for the first 25 frames in the sequence while
for the second band (frames 26 to 50) the quantity is zero which indicates that no
background modeling takes place for processing this band of frames and the old

background has been used for background subtraction. The results of only three out of the six videos are shown in Fig. 4.9 for the sake of clarity of the plot.

4.8 Analysis of Comparative Time and Space Complexity

This section analyzes the comparative analysis of time and space complexities of different methods. In the following discussion it is considered that each frame is of dimension MxN pixels containing a total $T = MxN \ pixels$

4.8.1 Stauffer-Grimson Method

The method proposed by Stauffer and Grimson [4] employs Gaussian Mixture Model (GMM) to extract pixel statistics towards modeling a background image. This method describes the probability of observing a certain pixel value at any time by means of a mixture of Gaussian distributions. Each Gaussian distribution is deemed to describe only one of the observable foreground or background objects. Background modeled by this method is having a complexity of $O(k)$ for modeling per pixel, where k is the number of Gaussian distributions used to model a pixel (typically in the order 3 to 5) [7].

Moreover, it is required to compute mean and standard deviation and computation of a Gaussian function for each pixel. This is an expensive operation in terms of number of computations. The assumption is that the higher and more compact the distribution, the more is likely to belong to the background. Therefore, distributions are ranked with respect to the peak amplitude and standard deviation; this requires sorting. In addition, the background update parameter is calculated based on last n frames and ranking. Detailed analysis of time and space complexities of this method is given below.

In finite mixture method, $f(x_i) = \{x_i \mid i = 1, 2 ..., n\}$ can be estimated as the sum of c weighted kernels as stated below

$$f(x) = \sum_{i=1}^{c} p_i g(x ; \theta_i), c \ll n$$

Where p_i denotes the weight for the i-th kernel, $\sum_{i=1}^{c} p_i, p_i \geq 0$, and $g(x ; \theta_i)$ is the probability density function with θ_i as the kernel density parameter. For each given vector x, it is considered as the background $f(x) > \tau$.

In the above equation, the parameter should be set in a way that higher value density function to be assigned to samples belonging to the background. Expectation maximization (EM) has been used as a tool for the optimization of the parameters. However, due to huge computations of EM, recursive computation technique has been employed as a better computationally effective solution for computing the following parameters:

$$w_{k+1} = (1-\alpha)\, w_k + \alpha \cdot p\left(k \mid x_t, \theta_k\right) \tag{4.1}$$

$$\mu_{k+1} = (1 - p_k)\, \mu_k + p_k x_t \tag{4.2}$$

$$\Sigma_{k+1} = (1 - p_k)\Sigma_k + p_k\left(x_t - \mu_{k+1}\right)\left(x_t - \mu_{k+1}\right)^T \tag{4.3}$$

$$\text{Where } \alpha = \frac{1}{N+1} \tag{4.4}$$

$$\text{and } p_k = \frac{\alpha \cdot p(k \mid x_t, \theta_k))}{w_k} \tag{4.5}$$

This algorithm has two phases: updating the parameters and the extraction of the moving objects. In the updating phase the mean, covariance and the coefficient associated with each kernel are updated. In addition there are a number of features (d) associated with each kernel.

Time Complexity In the updating phase, for each pixel, the weight, covariance and the coefficient parameters are to be computed. If data dimension is d, by assuming equal time consumption for multiplication and division and neglecting the time required for addition and subtraction; computation of weight (Eq. 4.1) will take $O(d*d)$, measurement of mean (Eq. 4.2) will take $O(d)$ and calculating the coefficient (Eq. 4.3) will account for $O(d*d)$ computations. Equation will take constant time $O(1)$ and Eq. 4.5 will cost $O(d*d)$ computations.

If the model makes use of k kernels, the updating phase will cost $O(k*d*d)$ for each pixel. For a frame size of MxN the time complexity of updating phase is $O(M*N*k*d*d)$.

In addition the extraction phase makes use of a kernel estimator function K using $Pr(x_i) = \frac{1}{N}\sum_{i=1}^{N} K(x - x_i)$. In the method proposed by Stauffer and Grimson, Gaussian probability density estimation has been used. This accounts for $O(k*d*d)$ computation per pixel making a total of $O(M*N*k*d*d)$ computation for a frame of dimension MxN.

Space Complexity The following assumptions are considered for analyzing the memory requirements:

Measurement of mean: If the dimension of the input data is d, then the dimension of mean vector is also d. A number of MxN pixels are considered for each frame. The number of kernels is k. Therefore, the memory requirement for measurement of mean is $O(k*M*N*d)$.

Measurement of covariance: If the number of dimensions is d, the size of the covariance matrix is dxd. The number of kernels for each pixel is k, therefore $k*d*d$ sized storage is required for each pixel. Therefore, for a single frame, the covariance measurement will take $O(M*N*d*d*k)$ space.

Measurement of coefficient: Each kernel requires one coefficient and there are k kernels associated with each pixel. Therefore, k coefficients are required for each pixel. The dimension of a frame is MxN leading to a memory requirement of $O(M*N*k)$ for each frame.

It is evident from the above discussion that the space complexity of the background updating phase of GMM is $O(M*N*d*d*k)$.

The second phase of GMM extracts the moving object. At this step, the values of mean, covariance and coefficient for each pixel are stored in the memory. According to the first phase the storage requirement for this step is also $O(M*N*d*d*k)$.

4.8.2 Pixel-based Adaptive Segmenter (PBAS)

Pixel-based Adaptive Segmenter (PBAS) method proposed by Hofmann et al. [5] follows a non-parametric paradigm. In this method, every pixel is modeled by an array of recently observed background values.

In PBAS the background model is generated by using k recently observed value of a pixel

$$B(x_i) = \{B_1(x_i), B_2(x_i), ... B_k(x_i)\} \tag{4.6}$$

A pixel x_i is decided to belong to the background if its pixel value $I(x_i)$ is closer than a certain decision threshold $R(x_i)$ to at $\#_{min}$ of the number k background values. The foreground segmentation mask is calculated as follows:

$$F(x_i) = 1, \; if \; \#\{dist(I(x_i), B_k(x_i)) < R(x_i)\} < \#_{min} \tag{4.7}$$

$$= 0, \; otherwise.$$

Here $F = 1$ represents foreground. It is seen that the decision making involves two parameters: (i) the decision threshold $R(x_i)$ which is defined for each pixel separately and (ii) minimum number $\#_{min}$ which is a fixed global parameter.

Time Complexity Let the background is modeled using previous k frames as suggested in Eq. 4.6. The generation of the foreground mask is an iterative process. It requires searching for the minimum distance between the set of all k pixels considered for background modeling to the intensity value of the particular pixel x_i in the current frame $I(x_i)$. This requires $O(k)$ computation per pixel. For a frame of size $T = MxN$, $O(Tk)$ computations are required. A typical value of k = 35 is suggested by the authors of the method [5]. The number of computations per frame is $O(Tk)$ which is quite high.

In addition, two controllers with feedback loops are used for setting a decision threshold $R(x_i)$ and a learning parameter $T(x_i)$ for background modeling.

To account for the background dynamics, the decision threshold $R(x_i)$ is calculated. In addition, updating decision parameter requires finding minimum distance contributing linear complexity in terms of number of pixels $B(x_i)$ being updated. An array of minimal decision distances are kept $D(x_i) = \{D_1(x_i), D_2(x_i), ... D_k(x_i)\}$.

During updating of $B_k(x_i)$ the following computations are made $d_{min}(x_i)$ = $min_k dist(I(x_i)x_i, B_k(x_i))$. The average of all such minimum distances are computed per pixel as a measure of background dynamics. This step accounts for $O(Tk)$ additional computations.

Afterwards the learning parameter $T(x_i)$ is computed to validate the background requiring additional computations. Updating learning rate involves calculating probability.

PBAS is a pixel based method in which the segmentation decision is made independently for each pixel. The output is generated by performing a spatial smoothing operation using median filtering. An empirical filter size of 9×9 is used in the post processing phase. The process is computationally intensive.

Space Complexity In PBAS the background model is generated by using k recently observed values of a pixel as $B(x_i) = \{B_1(x_i), B_2(x_i), ... B_k(x_i)\}$. For a frame size of MxN pixels, this step requires an auxiliary buffer of size $MxNxk$. Space complexity of this step is $O(M^*N^*k)$.

As shown in Eq. 4.7 a buffer of minimum decision distances are kept for a number of previous frames. This history is used in calculating the background dynamics and updating the decision threshold $R(x_i)$. This calls for additional storage requirement of $O(M^*N^*k)$.

4.8.3 Appearance Profile-based Spatio-temporal Method (KDE)

Pixel appearance profile-based spatio-temporal method proposed by Yoshinaga et al. [6] models the background considering the similarity of intensity changes among pixels using appearance profile of pixels. In particular, this method classifies pixels into several clusters, in each of which the appearance profiles of the pixels are similar. The foreground objects are detected based on the similarity of intensity changes between the target pixel and the cluster to which the target pixel belongs. The key idea of this method is based on the observation that most of the pixels belonging to the same cluster exhibit similar intensity changes against variations in illumination.

Time Complexity: Let C_k represent the number of pixels belonging to cluster k (a particular appearance profile pattern). Therefore, $C = \sum_{k=1}^{K} C_k$ where C is the total number of pixels for all the K clusters. The total number of computations done for all the clusters is $C = \sum_{k=1}^{K} C_k (C_k \log C_k + 2F_s)$. Here, F_s is the number of frames used for detection. In the worst case C $C = \sum_{k=1}^{K} C_k (C_k \log C_k + 2F_s) < C^2 \log C + 2CF_s \approx O(C^2 \log C)$.

It is assumed that the total number of pixels in a frame is $T=MxN$. T=C=total number of pixels for all the clusters. Therefore the time complexity can be expressed as $O(T^2 \log T)$. The time complexity is quadratic in nature. This implies for a considerably large frame size, the number of computations required for processing is prohibitive due to huge number of computations.

Space Complexity This method is divided into two major steps:clustering based on appearance profile and object detection using similarity of appearance profile. In terms of space complexity, the most expensive step is the one that finds out the changing trend of pixels. In this step, the pixels are grouped into several clusters based on the similarity of their intensity changes in a certain short period. A short-term intensity change is defined as $S=\{i_1, i_2, \ldots \ldots i_k\}$, considering past k frames in the sequence of frames. This step requires a buffer size of $O(k)$ per pixel. Therefore, for a frame of size MxN, $O(M*N*k)$ space is required.

Auxiliary storage requirements of other steps are smaller than $O(M*N*k)$. Therefore, the space complexity of this method is $O(M*N*k)$.

4.8.4 The Proposed Method

This section briefly describes the time and space complexities of the proposed method.

Time Complexity The time complexity of the proposed method is explained as follows:Let R be the number of frames considered for background modeling. The median of all the pixel values of last R frames are to be computed. A comparison based sorting requires $O(Rlog(R))$comparisons for each pixel. However, the intensity values range from 0–255, therefore a linear sorting method like counting sort can be applied reducing the time complexity to $O(R)$ only. A total of T pixels to be processed totaling TR computations $\approx O(TR) \approx O(T)$, as $R << T$.

Block processing requires computation of the similarity coefficient. Considering each block containing $N'=mxn$ pixels; a total of B blocks are to be processed per frame. Computation of the similarity coefficient mostly contains additions and subtractions. There are three multiplications associated with each pixel for computation of block similarity coefficient. A total of $3N'$numbers of multiplications are required per block. For B blocks, the total number of computations is $3N'B$, i.e. linear in N' $\approx T$ i.e. $O(T)$ as $B << N'$ and $N' << T$.

Let S be the number of frames used for computing block statistics. Let D be the total number of foreground pixels detected in block processing step. The background subtraction step mainly involves computing the mean, standard deviation and maximum and minimum intensity levels of past S frames for each of D pixels. Computing mean involves mostly additions suggesting total number of computations is SD, i.e., linear with respect to D. Standard Deviation requires S number of multiplications, a total of SD computations, i.e. linear in D. Computing minimum and maximum needs approximately SD computations, linear with respect to D. Complexity of background subtraction step is $O(SD) \approx O(T)$ as $S << D << T$.

The post processing step finds out the blobs from the foreground mask by a two pass method. This requires two-passes to iterate through the 2-dimensional binary mask of size MxN. This can be efficiently implemented using union-find data-structures.

Overall time complexity of the proposed method is $O(T)+O(T)+O(T)$ $\approx kT \approx O(T)$. The value of the constant multiplier k is small. This shows that the

Table 4.2 Comparative Performance Analysis

Method	Time	Space	Comment
Stauffer-Grimson (GMM)	$O(M*N*k*d*d)$	$O(M*N*d*d*k)$	k = number of kernels per pixel, d = number of features associated with each kernel. In terms of both time and space complexities, GMM is expensive compared to the proposed method.
Pixel-based Adapter Segmenter (PBAS)	$O(M*N*k)$	$O(M*N*k)$	Both time and space complexities are linear in terms of $T = MxN$. In case of time complexity, the value of the constant multiplier k in PBAS is much higher than that of the proposed method. Space complexity of PBAS is comparable with that of the proposed method.
KDE Spatio-temporal	$O(T^2 logT)$	$O(M*N*k)$	Here $T = MxN$. Time complexity is quadratic in T. Space complexity is linear with respect to T. Space complexity of KDE is comparable with that of the proposed method.
Proposed	$O(M*N*k)$	$O(M*N*k)$	Both time and space complexities are linear in terms of number of pixels present per frame. The value of the constant multiplier associated with Big-Oh is small.

proposed method makes less number of computations compared to the other three methods for modeling and subtracting the background.

Space Complexity: Background modeling is done using *median* of grayscale intensities of each pixel on last k frames. Background frame at time t for a particular pixel x (denoted as x_t) is calculated as follows: $BG(x_t) = median\{x_i \mid i = m_1 to m_2\}$; where $m_1 = t - k - bg\_offset$ to $m_2 = t - bg\_offset$

This step requires a buffer of size k per pixel. If the dimension of a frame is MxN pixels, a buffer of size $MxNxk$ pixels is required by the background modeling step.

Block processing requires storing and comparing the modeled background frame and the current frame. This requires a buffer of size of no more than $2xMxN$ pixels.

Block statistics are computed only for the pixels detected as *changed* in the block processing step. The number of pixels for which block statistics are to be computed (let us say D) are very less compared to the total number of pixels in a frame ($T=MxN$). Let S number of frames is considered for computing the block statistics requiring a buffer of size SxD. It is obvious that $S << D << T$.

The post processing step works on the binary mask of size MxN. Therefore, the background modeling step is taking the maximum auxiliary storage space which is of size $MxNxk$. Therefore, the space complexity of the proposed method is $O(M*N*k)$.

Table 4.2 summarizes whatever is discussed in this subsection.

It is obvious from the above discussion that the proposed method is less costly in terms of both time complexity and storage requirements compared to other methods. Moreover, it is also worth mentioning that in the proposed method, the background

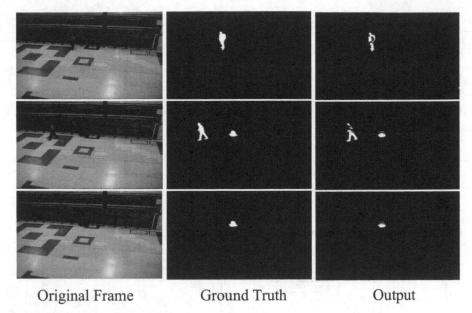

Original Frame   Ground Truth   Output

Fig. 4.10 Foreground object detection

is not updated for every frame in the sequence. This saves huge time and space in detecting foreground moving objects. This suggests that in practical scenarios the proposed method will work much efficiently compared to other methods.

This methodology for moving object detection has been documented in [8].

4.9   Surveillance Application: A Case Study

The performance of the proposed method is tested on the benchmark surveillance video dataset provided by Performance Evaluation of Tracking and Surveillance (PETS2006) [9]. The resolution of all sequences is PAL standard (768×576 pixels, 25 frames per second) and compressed as JPEG image sequences. Video is captured from multiple cameras. In this experiment, the video captured by camera-3 is considered. This video contains a surveillance video sequence captured in a station with multiple moving objects (human being) passing to and fro in a station. This also depicts an abandoned bag situation which may be a possible security threat.

PETS2006 dataset comes along with the set of ground truth images for quantitative evaluation. A set of 1200 frames sequence is considered for testing.

Results of the proposed method are compared with the provided ground truth images on the basis of the evaluation metrics stated in Sect. 4.4.

A set of three frames are shown in Fig. 4.10. The first column shows the original frame; in the second column the corresponding ground-truth images are presented. The third column presents the output of the proposed method.

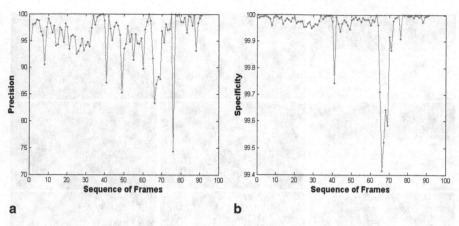

Fig. 4.11 Performance evaluation. (**a**) Precision (**b**) Specificity

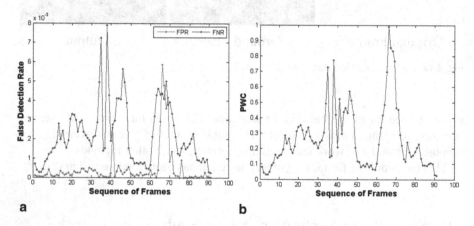

Fig. 4.12 Performance evaluation. (**a**) FPR and FNR (**b**) PWC

A study is made to check for the accuracy of recognition of the proposed method. Results are shown in Fig. 4.11 and Fig. 4.12.

In Fig. 4.11 two plots are presented. Figure 4.11 (a) shows the results on the basis of precision measure for a set of 900 frames (samples are taken 10 frames apart). It is found that more than 90 % precision is obtained for most of the frames. In Fig. 4.11 (b) the results of the same set of frames are shown for the specificity measure. A total of 99 % scores of specificity are obtained for all the frames.

In Fig. 4.12 (a) false detection rate is plotted against the number of frames. The red line shows the false positive rate (FPR) and the blue line depicts the false negative rate (FNR) obtained for a set of 900 frames (the samples are taken 10 frames apart). A plot of the percentage of wrong classification (PWC) is presented in Fig. 4.12 (b) for the same set of frames. Results show that the values of PWC are quite small which is desired.

Results depicted in Fig. 4.11 and Fig. 4.12 show the effectiveness of the proposed method in terms of accuracy of detection of the moving objects.

This study shows an application of the proposed background subtraction method in the context of processing a surveillance video for moving object detection. This case study along with the results of this subsection has been reported in [10].

4.10   Conclusions

In this chapter, a novel background subtraction method is presented for detecting moving objects under dynamic background conditions. The method involves block processing in which a significant portion of the present frame is discarded from further consideration in subsequent background subtraction step. Pixel statistics are computed only for the regions of the frames that qualify as changed during block processing. This step reduces the amount of data to be processed and hence saves significant processing time. This method is low-cost in terms of computational complexity as well as storage requirements compared to other recent background subtraction methods. Comparative performance analysis on standard benchmark dataset shows that even though the method is of low cost, it produces very competitive results with other state-of-the-art methods. Low computational complexity makes it suitable to be used in practical applications for resource constrained devices. The effectiveness of the proposed method is also verified on a standard surveillance video.

Bibliography

1. R. Cucchiara, C. Grana, M. Piccardi, A. Prati; "Detecting moving objects, ghosts, and shadows in video streams", IEEE Transactions on Pattern Analysis and Machine Intelligence, Vol. 25 (10), pp. 1337–1342, 2003.
2. N. Goyette, P.-M. Jodoin, F. Porikli, J. Konrad, P. Ishwar; "changedetection.net: A new change detection benchmark dataset", IEEE Workshop on Change Detection (CDW), pp. 16–21, 2012.
3. C. Stauffer, W. E. L. Grimson; "Learning patterns of activity using real-time tracking", IEEE Transactions on Pattern Analysis and Machine Intelligence, Vol. 22 (8). pp. 747–757, 2000.
4. C. Stauffer, W. E. L. Grimson; "Adaptive background mixture models for real-time tracking", IEEE Int. Conf. on Computer Vision and Pattern Recognition (CVPR), Vol. 2, 1999.
5. M. Hofmann, P.Tiefenbacher, G. Rigoll; "Background Segmentation with Feedback: The Pixel-Based Adaptive Segmenter", IEEE Workshop on Change Detection, pp. 38–43, 2012.
6. S. Yoshinaga, A. Shimada, H. Nagahara, Rin-ichiro Taniguchi; "Background Model Based on Intensity Change Similarity Among Pixels", 19th Japan-Korea Joint Workshop on Frontiers of Computer Vision, pp. 276–280, 2013.

7. M. Piccardi, "Background subtraction techniques: A review", IEEE Int. Conf on Systems, Man and Cybernetics (SMC), Vol. 4, pp. 3199–3104, 2004.
8. S.H.Shaikh, K. Saeed and N. Chaki; "A new background subtraction method towards moving object detection for dynamic scenes"; Submitted to the Journal of Pattern Recognition and Image Analysis, February, 2014.
9. PETS 2006: Banchmark Dataset: 9th IEEE International Workshop on Performance Evaluation of Tracking and Surveillance; http://www.cvg.rdg.ac.uk/PETS2006/data.html
10. S. H. Shaikh, K. Saeed, N. Chaki; "Moving Object Detection in Surveillance Video using Background Subtraction"; Presented in the PhD Symposium of the 9th International Conference on Information Systems Security (ICISS) held in Indian Statistical Institute (ISI), Kolkata, December 2013.

Chapter 5
Databases for Research

This chapter summarizes some of the databases available for research for moving object detection, tracking and activity classification. The following subsections contain brief descriptions of the databases along with sample video frames taken from them.

5.1 ViSOR (Video Surveillance Online Repository)

ViSOR contains a large set of multimedia data and the corresponding annotations. The repository has been conceived as a support tool for different research projects. Together with the videos, ViSOR contains metadata annotation; both manually annotated ground-truth data and automatically obtained outputs of a particular system. In such a manner, the users of the repository are able to perform validation tasks of their own algorithms as well as comparative activities.

This dataset contains a couple of videos (e.g. videos of construction working sites, outdoor video with shadows, video for indoor people tracking with occlusions, traffic surveillance, human action recognition for the purpose of surveillance, stopped vehicles detection etc.) for performance evaluation (Fig. 5.1).

5.2 ETISEO

ETISEO is a Video Understanding Evaluation project a part of the Techno-Vision evaluation network funded by the French ministry of defense and the French ministry of research. ETISEO focuses on the treatment and interpretation of videos involving pedestrians and (or) vehicles, indoors or outdoors, obtained from fixed cameras. The data is hosted by INRIA Sophia Antipolis. The resources generated during the project—videos, ground-truth, and evaluation tools are made public for use of research.

S. H. Shaikh et al., *Moving Object Detection Using Background Subtraction*,
SpringerBriefs in Computer Science, DOI 10.1007/978-3-319-07386-6_5,
© The Author(s) 2014

Fig. 5.1 ViSOR Dataset. **a** Shadows, **b** Traffic Surveillance, **c** Stopped vehicle detection, **d** Background Modeling video. (Source: ViSOR repository: http://www.openvisor.org [1])

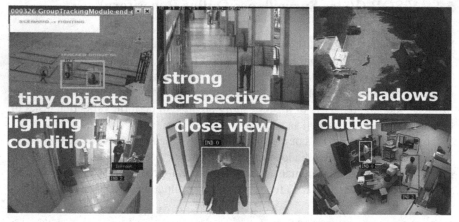

Fig. 5.2 ETISEO: Different scenarios for performance evaluation tiny objects, strong perspective, shadows, different lighting conditions, close view, clutter. (Source: ETISEO: http://www-sop. inria.fr/orion/ETISEO/index.htm [2])

This dataset contains more than 80 video clippings of various indoor and outdoor scenes. Since the ground truth consists mainly of high-level information such as the bounding box, object class, event type, etc., this dataset is more suitable for tracking, classification and event recognition than change detection.

The various scenarios considered are the following: tiny objects, strong perspective, shadows, different lighting conditions, close view, clutter (Fig. 5.2).

a   b   c

Fig. 5.3 SABS Dataset. **a** Ground-truth annotation, **b** An artificial frame, **c** Shadow annotation. (Source:http://www.vis.uni-stuttgart.de/forschung/informationsvisualisierung-und-visual-analytics/visuelle-analyse-videostroeme/sabs.html [3])

5.3 SABS Dataset

The SABS (Stuttgart Artificial Background Subtraction) dataset is an artificial dataset for pixel-wise evaluation of background models. The use of artificial data enables judge the performance of background subtraction methods for each of the challenges background subtraction has to cope with. Realistic video footage was created using ray-tracing technology with global illumination. Sensor noise was simulated using additive Gaussian noise. In contrast to manually annotated ground-truth data, the SABS dataset does not suffer from imperfect labels or only a small number of annotated frames.

The following typical challenges of background subtraction in the context of video surveillance have been addressed in the evaluation: gradual illumination changes, sudden illumination changes, dynamic background, camouflage, shadows, bootstrapping and video noise (Fig. 5.3).

5.4 Wallflower

This dataset contains the test images to be used for testing several different background maintenance algorithms on seven different image sequences. Ground-truth images are provided in the form of binary masks segmenting the background and foreground pixels. Each of the video is representing a specific challenge such as illumination change, background motion, etc. Only one frame per video has been labeled in this dataset (Fig. 5.4).

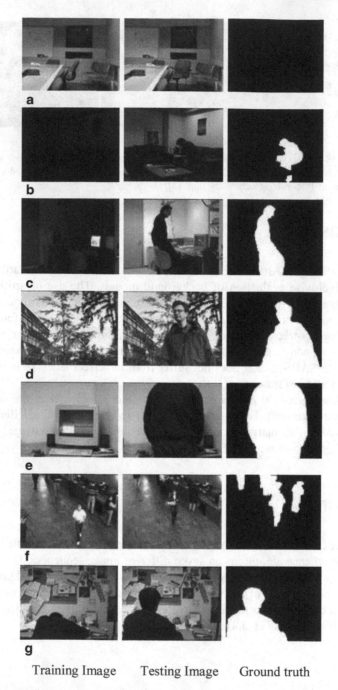

Training Image   Testing Image   Ground truth

Fig. 5.4 Test scenarios from Wallflower dataset. **a** Moved Object, **b** Time of Day, **c** Light Switch, **d** Waving Trees, **e** Camouflage, **f** Bootstrapping, **g** Foreground Aperture. (Source: http://research. microsoft.com/en-us/um/people/jckrumm/WallFlower/TestImages.htm [4])

5.5 LIMU (Laboratory for Image and Media Understanding)

This database is provided by the Department of Advanced Information Technology, Kyushu University, Japan. It includes some ground truth dataset to evaluate the result of moving object detection. Apart from ground-truth (15 frames apart) of PETS 2001 (with and without shadow) it also provides benchmark data considering indoor scene with camera parameter changes, on/off light switches, data varying over time in outdoor (bus stop during morning and evening), traffic intersection. In object based ground truth, objects are painted in different colors. Each object keeps its color if it appears for several frames (Fig. 5.5).

5.6 UCSD

This database is provided by the Statistical Visual Computing Laboratory, University of California, San Diego. The dataset consists of 18 video sequences. The frames of each sequence are provided in JPEG format. The ground-truth masks are also provided (Fig. 5.6).

5.7 MTA SZTAKI

Hungarian Academy of Sciences Institute for Computer Science and Control

This benchmark set contains raw video frames and binary foreground respectively shadow ground truth masks (drawn by hand), which were used for validation. The three sequences (Seam, Sepm, Senoon) are outdoor surveillance videos which were captured and evaluated by the employees of the MTA-SZTAKI (Fig. 5.7).

Ground-truth is not provided for all the frames. Sequences SEAM, SEPM and SENOON contain ground-truth for 160, 75, 251 frames respectively.

5.8 PETS (Performance Evaluation of Tracking and Surveillance) Dataset

PETS 2000 Outdoor people and vehicle tracking (single camera). Two sequences: (a) training sequence of 3672 frames at 25 Hz (146.88 s) and (b) test sequence of 1452 frames (58.08 s). The sequences are available in 2 formats: (a) QuickTime movie format with Motion JpegA compression; individual Jpeg files for training and testing are also provided. No ground-truth frame is included in this set (Fig. 5.8).

PETS 2001 Outdoor people and vehicle tracking (two synchronized views; includes omni-directional and moving camera). PETS 2001 consists of five separate sets of

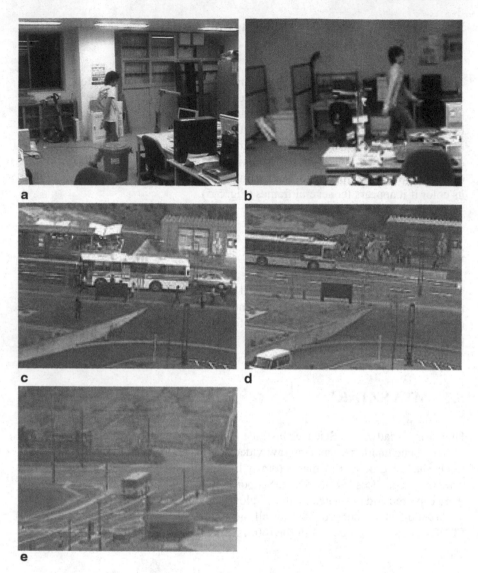

Fig. 5.5 a Changing camera parameters in indoor scenes. **b** Indoor Switch on/off. **c** Bus Stop in the Morning. **d** Bus Stop in the Evening. **e** Traffic Intersection. (Source: LIMU; http://limu.ait. kyushu-u.ac.jp/dataset/en/ [5])

training and test sequences, i.e. each set consists of one training sequence and one test sequence. All the datasets are multi-view (2 cameras) and are significantly more challenging than for PETS'2000 in terms of significant lighting variation, occlusion, scene activity and use of multi-view data. Ground-truth images are provided in the form of centroid and bounding box coordinates on image plane, object class (person, vehicle, other), position on ground plane and object orientation.

Fig. 5.6 Some of the test videos of UCSD Dataset. **a** Surf, **b** Flock, **c** Boat, **d** Bottle, **e** Freeway, **f** Peds. (Source: UCSD http://www.svcl.ucsd.edu/projects/background_subtraction/ucsdbgsub_dataset.htm [6])

VS-PETS 2003-INMOVE Outdoor people tracking—football data (three synchronized views). The datasets consists of football players moving around a pitch.

PETS 2006 ISCAPS Surveillance of public spaces, detection of left luggage events. Scenarios of increasing complexity captured using multiple sensors. The data is captured at 25 frames per second. The resolution is 768×576. The videos are available either as *MPEG's* or as a numbered set of *JPEG* image files

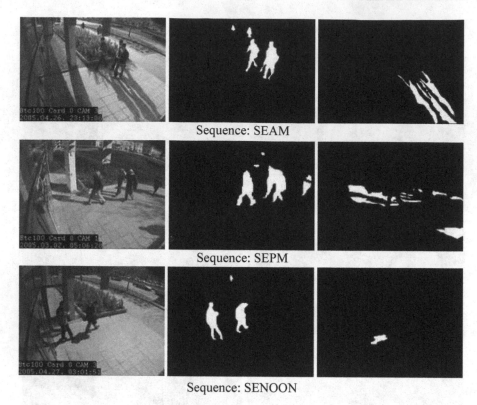

Sequence: SEAM

Sequence: SEPM

Sequence: SENOON

Raw Frame   Foreground Ground-truth   Shadow Ground-truth

Fig. 5.7 SZTAKI Benchmark set. (Source: http://web.eee.sztaki.hu/~bcsaba/FgShBenchmark. html [7, 8])

PETS 2007 REASON Dataset The datasets are multi-sensor sequences containing the following 3 scenarios, with increasing scene complexity: (1) loitering, (2) attended luggage removal (theft), (3) Un-attended luggage.

5.9 BEHAVE Dataset [49]

The dataset comprises of two views of various scenario's of people acting out various interactions. Ten basic scenarios were acted out. These were called InGroup (IG), Approach (A), WalkTogether (WT), Split (S), Ignore (I), Following (FO), Chase (C), Fight (FI), RunTogether (RT), and Meet (M).The data is captured at 25 frames per second. The resolution is 640 × 480. The videos are available either as AVI's or as a numbered set of JPEG single image files (Fig. 5.9).

Fig. 5.8 PETS Dataset. **a** PETS 2000, **b** PETS 2001, **c** VS-PETS 2003 INMOVE, **d** PETS 2006 ISCAPS, **e** PETS 2007 REASON. (Source: http://www.cvg.rdg.ac.uk/slides/pets.html [9])

5.10   Change Detection Dataset

There are two datasets providing realistic, camera-captured diverse set of videos. The videos included cover a wide range of detection challenges and are representative of typical indoor and outdoor visual data captured nowadays in surveillance, smart environment, and video database scenarios.

2012-DATASET consists of 31 camera-captured videos (approximately 70,000 frames) spanning 6 categories selected to include diverse change and motion detection challenges:

Baseline category represents a mixture of mild challenges typical of the next 4 categories. Some videos have subtle background motion, others have isolated shadows, some have an abandoned object and others have pedestrians that stop for a short while and then move away. These videos are fairly easy, but not trivial, to process, and are provided mainly as reference (Fig. 5.10).

Dynamic Background category includes scenes with strong (parasitic) background motion: boats on shimmering water, cars passing next to a fountain, or pedestrians, cars and trucks passing in front of a tree shaken by the wind.

Camera Jitter category contains indoor and outdoor videos captured by unstable (e.g., vibrating) cameras. The jitter magnitude varies from one video to another.

Intermittent Object Motion category includes videos with scenarios known for causing "ghosting" artifacts in the detected motion, i.e., objects move, then stop for a short while, after which they start moving again. Some videos include still objects that suddenly start moving, e.g., a parked vehicle driving away, and also abandoned objects. This category is intended for testing how various algorithms adapt to background changes.

Shadows category consists of indoor and outdoor videos exhibiting strong as well as faint shadows. Some shadows are fairly narrow while others occupy most

a   b

Fig. 5.10 Change Detection Dataset. **a** Original Frame, **b** Ground-truth. (Source: http://www.changedetection.net/ [11])

of the scene. Also, some shadows are cast by moving objects while others are cast by trees and buildings.

Thermal category includes videos that have been captured by far-infrared cameras. These videos contain typical thermal artifacts such as heat stamps (e.g., bright spots left on a seat after a person gets up and leaves), heat reflection on floors and windows, and camouflage effects, when a moving object has the same temperature as the surrounding regions.

Accurate ground truths are made publicly available for testing and evaluation for all the frames of all the videos in all six video categories of the 2012-DATASET.

2014-DATASET includes all the videos from the 2012-DATASET plus 22 additional camera-captured videos (approximately 70,000 new frames) spanning 5 new categories that incorporate challenges that were not addressed in the 2012-DATASET:

Challenging Weather: This category includes outdoor videos captured in challenging winter weather conditions, i.e., snow storm, snow on the ground, fog.

Low Frame-Rate: This category contains videos capture at varying frame-rates between 0.17 fps and 1 fps.

Night: This category includes videos captured at night (difficult light conditions) of, primarily, motor traffic.

PTZ: This category contains video footage captured by pan-tilt-zoom cameras in slow continuous pan mode, intermittent pan mode, 2-position patrol-mode PTZ, or zooming-in/zooming-out

Air Turbulence: This category includes outdoor videos showing air turbulence caused by rising heat.

In addition, whereas ground truths for all frames were made publicly available for the 2012-DATASET for testing and evaluation, in the 2014-DATASET, ground truths of only the first half of every video in the 5 new categories is made publicly available for testing.

The videos have been obtained with different cameras ranging from low-resolution IP cameras, through mid-resolution camcorders and PTZ cameras, to far- and near-infrared cameras. As a consequence, spatial resolutions of the videos vary from 320×240 to 720×576. Also, due to diverse lighting conditions present and compression parameters used, the level of noise and compression artifacts varies from one video to another. The length of the videos also varies from 1000 to 8000 frames and the videos shot by low-end IP cameras suffer from noticeable radial distortion. Different cameras may have different hue bias (due to different white balancing algorithms employed) and some cameras apply automatic exposure adjustment resulting in global brightness fluctuations in time. The frame rate also varies from one video to another, often due to a limited bandwidth.

5.11 CAVIAR (Context Aware Vision using Image-based Active Recognition)

The main objective of CAVIAR was to utilize rich local image descriptions towards improving image-based recognition processes. This is clearly addressing issues central to the cognitive vision approach.

The two major applications that CAVIAR addresses were- i) City centre surveillance: Many large cities have nighttime crime and antisocial behaviour problems, such as drunkenness, fights, vandalism, breaking and entering shop windows, etc. Often these cities have video cameras already installed, but what is lacking is a semi-automatic analysis of the video stream. Such analysis could detect unusual events, such as patterns of running people, converging people, or stationary people, and then alert human security staff. ii) Marketers are interested in the behaviour of potential customers in a commercial setting, such as what sequence of locations do they visit, how long they stop at particular locations, what behavioural options do typical customers take, etc. Automatic analysis of customer behaviour could enable evaluation of shop layouts, changing displays and the effect of promotional materials.

A number of video clippings were recorded for the CAVIAR project acting out the different scenarios of interest. These include people walking alone, meeting with others, window shopping, entering and exiting shops, fighting and passing out and leaving a package in a public place.

One set of videos of this project were captured in the INRIA Labs at Grenoble, France. The resolution is half-resolution PAL standard (384×288 pixels, 25 frames per second) and compressed using MPEG2. The ground truth for these sequences was found by hand-labeling the images.

A typical frame from the image sequences is given in Fig. 5.11a. It shows three individual boxes (yellow) and one group box (green). There are several people in the video sequence that are not boxed because they do not move over the course of the sequence.

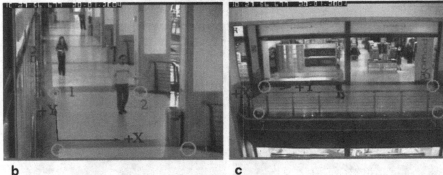

Fig. 5.11 CAVIAR Dataset. **a** Individual and group, **b** Corridor View, **c** Front. (Source: EC Funded CAVIAR project/IST 2001 37540, found at URL: http://homepages.inf.ed.ac.uk/rbf/CAVIAR/ [12])

In another set of experiments, each clipping was recorder from two different points of view (Fig. 5.11b and c). The first one shows a view of the corridor, while the second shows a frontal view of the scenario. The two video sequences should be time synchronized frame by frame. However, each video set may start at slightly different times, therefore frame correspondences may be necessary.

5.12   Imagery Library for Intelligent Detection Systems (i-LIDS)

The Imagery Library for Intelligent Detection Systems (i-LIDS) is the government's benchmark for video analytics (VA) systems. It has been developed by the Centre for Applied Science and Technology (CAST) in partnership with the Centre for the Protection of National Infrastructure (CPNI). i-LIDS comprises a library of CCTV

Fig. 5.12 i-LIDS Dataset. **a** Abandoned Package, **b** Doorway Surveillance, **c** Parked Vehicle, **d** Sterile Zone, (Source: https://www.gov.uk/imagery-library-for-intelligent-detection-systems [13])

video footage based around 'scenarios' central to the government's requirements. The footage accurately represents real operating conditions and potential threats.

i-LIDS currently has the following datasets available for distribution and evaluation.

Event detection scenarios: sterile zone, parked vehicle, abandoned baggage, doorway surveillance and new technologies.

Tracking scenario: multiple camera tracking has been considered.

The datasets for these scenarios are available in training and test formats. The datasets for the event detection scenarios each contain approximately 24 h of footage. Each of these datasets is filmed to represent all weather conditions, time of day and scene densities expected within the scenario. The multiple camera tracking scenario datasets each contain approximately 50 h of real world footage.

Each dataset consists of 2 or 3 camera views, referred to as stages, and is further segmented into shorter video clips of 30 to 60 min. The training dataset is further split into individual events (Fig. 5.12).

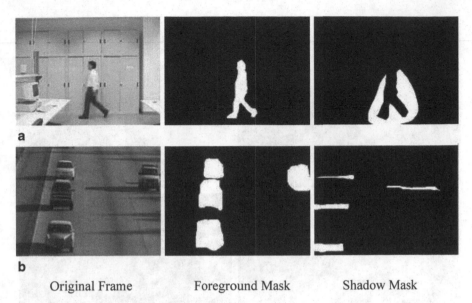

Original Frame	Foreground Mask	Shadow Mask

Fig. 5.13 ATON Benchmark Set. **a** Laboratory Sequence, **b** Highway Sequence. (Source: http://cvrr.ucsd.edu/aton/shadow/ [14])

5.13   ATON

Detection of shadows of moving objects is an important research aspect. In ATON project detection and analysis of shadows is an important research thrust.

The following figure shows two ('Laboratory', 'Highway') videos from ATON benchmark set (Fig. 5.13).

5.14   Image Sequences from Karlsruhe University database

This dataset contains a number of gray-value images of different traffic intersections in various format (GIF, PGM, PPM etc.) in different dimensions (512×512, 720×576, 740×560, 702×566, 688×565, 256×191)(Fig. 5.14).

Fig. 5.14 Karlsruhe University Database. (Karlsruhe Image Sequences. http://i21www.ira.uka.de/image_sequences/ [15])

Bibliography

1. ViSOR: R. Vezzani, R. Cucchiara, "Video Surveillance Online Repository (ViSOR): an integrated framework", Multimedia Tools and Applications, Vol. 50 (2), pp. 359–380, 2010.
2. ETISEO: http://www-sop.inria.fr/orion/ETISEO/index.htm; Accessed: March 2014.
3. SABS: Brutzer, Sebastian; Höferlin, Benjamin; Heidemann, Gunther; "Evaluation of Background Subtraction Techniques for Video Surveillance", Computer Vision and Pattern Recognition (CVPR), pp. 1937–1944, 2011.
4. Wallflower: Kentaro Toyama, John Krumm, Barry Brumitt, Brian Meyers, "Wallflower: Principles and Practice of Background Maintenance", Seventh International Conference on Computer Vision, pp. 255–261, 1999.
5. LIMU (Laboratory for Image and Media Understanding); URL: http://limu.ait.kyushu-u.ac.jp/dataset/en/; Accessed: March 2014.
6. UCSD: V. Mahadevan and N. Vasconcelos: Spatiotemporal Saliency in Highly Dynamic Scenes, IEEE Trans. on Pattern Analysis and Machine Intelligence, Vol. 32 (1), pp. 171–177, 2010.
7. MTA SZTAKI: Cs. Benedek and T. Szirányi: "Bayesian Foreground and Shadow Detection in Uncertain Frame Rate Surveillance Videos", IEEE Transactions on Image Processing, Vol. 17(4), pp. 608–621, 2008.
8. MTA SZTAKI: Cs. Benedek and T. Szirányi: "Study on Color Space Selection for Detecting Cast Shadows in Video Surveillance," International Journal of Imaging Systems and Technology, Special Issue on Applied Color Image Processing, Vol. 17(3), pp. 190–201, Wiley, 2007.

9. PETS (Performance Evaluation of Tracking and Surveillance) Dataset; URL: http://www.cvg.rdg.ac.uk/slides/pets.html; Accessed: March 2014.
10. BEHAVE: URL: http://groups.inf.ed.ac.uk/vision/BEHAVEDATA/INTERACTIONS/index.html; Accessed: March 2014.
11. Change Detection, Dataset; URL: http://www.changedetection.net/; Accessed: March 2014.
12. CAVIAR (Context Aware Vision using Image-based Active Recognition), EC Funded project/IST 2001 37540, URL: http://homepages.inf.ed.ac.uk/rbf/CAVIAR/; Accessed: March 2014.
13. Imagery Library for Intelligent Detection Systems (i-LIDS); URL: https://www.gov.uk/imagery-library-for-intelligent-detection-systems; Accessed: March 2014.
14. ATON: A. Prati, I. Mikiæ, M. Trivedi, R. Cucchiara, "Detecting Moving Shadows: Formulation, Algorithms and Evaluation", IEEE. Trans. Pattern Analysis and Machine Intelligence, Vol. 25(7), 2003.
15. Karlsruhe University, Image Sequences; http://i21www.ira.uka.de/image_sequences/; Accessed: March 2014.

Chapter 6
Conclusions

Moving object detection and tracking has a wide variety of applications in computer vision such as video surveillance and monitoring, video compression, vision-based control systems, human-computer interfaces, medical image processing, virtual and augmented reality, robotics etc. Moreover, this technique provides input to higher level vision-based tasks, such as representation and reconstruction of 3D images. It also plays an important role in content-based indexing and retrieval in video databases. These have been discussed in Chap. 1 for video processing along with object detection and tracking.

Chapter 2 of the text presents an overview of different techniques for moving object detection from video, namely background subtraction, temporal differencing, statistical methods and optical flow. This chapter also states some of the challenges faced by researchers in computer vision-based moving object detection. All of the common challenging aspects have been given in this chapter in detail with emphasis on: illumination changes, dynamic background, presence of shadows, motion of the camera, video noise, speed of the moving objects and the challenging weather conditions.

In Chap. 3, a brief review of the literature on the existing techniques on moving object detection is presented. The state-of-the-art review finds that there still exists gaps in devising some effective ways of removing background from an image.

Chapter 4 presents a new method for moving object detection using background subtraction for dynamic scenes. The method is tested on a benchmark video data set. The new approache has been discussed with examples and the results are presented to the readers. Comparative quantitative performance analysis reveals the effectiveness of the new method compared to someother standard methods in the literature.

Chapter 5 summarizes some of the widely used benchmark public databases for research in moving object detection, tracking and activity recognition.

However, the subject of detection and tracking of objects from video in a robust manner and in real time is still a open research problem. It needs improvement in the state-of-the-art technology towards a practical, automated and robust way to overcome the typical challenges and problems related to background subtraction in the context of video surveillance. Research is still going on towards a better method that handles all types of real-life problems associated with the same.

S. H. Shaikh et al., *Moving Object Detection Using Background Subtraction*,
SpringerBriefs in Computer Science, DOI 10.1007/978-3-319-07386-6_6,
© The Author(s) 2014